THE PORT CHICAGO MUTINY

ROBERT L. ALLEN

THE PORT CHICAGO MUTINY

WARNER BOOKS

A Warner Communications Company

AN AMISTAD BOOK

Warner Books, Inc., 666 Fifth Avenue, New York, NY 10103

W A Warner Communications Company

Printed in the United States of America
First printing: March 1989
10 9 8 7 6 5 4 3 2 1

Library of Congress Cataloging-in-Publication Data

Allen, Robert L., 1942–
    The Port Chicago mutiny / Robert L. Allen.
        p. 192
    1. Port Chicago Mutiny, Port Chicago, Calif., 1944—non-fiction.
2. World War, 1939–1945—Participation, Afro-American—non-fiction.
3. World War, 1939–1945—California—non-fiction.   4. Afro-Americans—
California—History—non-fiction.   5. World War, 1939–1945—non-fiction.
I. Title.
PS3551.L416P6 1989
813'.54—dc19   88-23667
ISBN 0-446-71004-0   CIP

Designed by Giorgetta Bell McRee

This book is dedicated with love to my son,
CASEY DOUGLASS ALLEN

CONTENTS

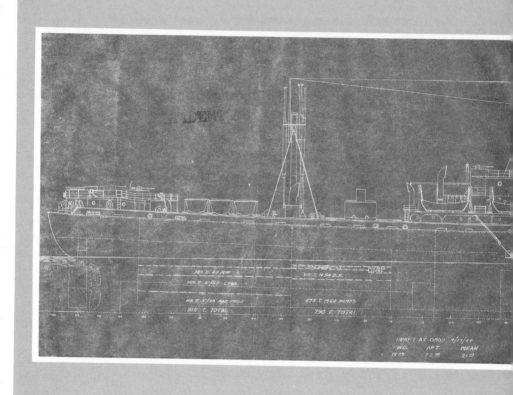

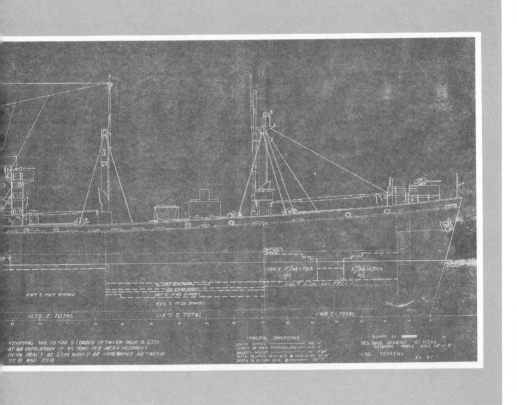

ASSUMING 300 TO 500 T. LOADED BETWEEN 0800 & 2213
AT AN IMMERSION OF 45 TONS PER INCH = PROBABLE
MEAN DRAFT AT 2213 WOULD BE SOMEWHERE BETWEEN
22 2¹ AND 22 8⁹

PRINCIPAL DIMENSIONS

DES. BASE DRAWING   NO. 10268
OUTBOARD   PROFILE   SCALE 1/8"=1'-0"

U.S.S.   SERPENS   AK 97

mutiny?

**The real story of how the Navy branded
50 fear-shocked sailors as mutineers**

Cover of pamphlet published in 1945 to publicize case of Port Chicago men.
Men in photo are handling canisters of ammunition.

ACKNOWLEDGMENTS

Many people aided me in the research and writing of this book. In particular I would like to express my appreciation to the following individuals and institutions for their assistance in locating primary documentary sources: William Heimdahl, Archivist, Navy and Old Army Branch, National Archives, Washington, D.C.; Clifford Kudo, Office of the Judge Advocate General, U.S. Navy, Washington, D.C.; Sylvia Render, Manuscript Historian, Manuscript Division, Library of Congress, Washington, D.C.; Ruth Nicholson, Librarian, Manuscript Division, Library of Congress, Washington, D.C.; Dean C. Allard, Head, Operational Archives, U.S. Navy History Division, Washington Navy Yard, Washington, D.C.; Donna Gloeckner, Librarian, NAACP Legal Defense and Educational Fund, New York; James Otsuki and Kathleen O'Connor, Archivists, Federal Record Center, San Bruno, California; Julie Streets, Archivist, Bureau of Yards and Docks Archives, U.S. Navy, Port Hueneme, California; and Kerstin Lucid of San Francisco.

For oral history materials I am deeply grateful to the Port Chicago survivors who consented to be interviewed, especially Joseph R. Small. I also thank the Bureau of Personnel of the Navy Department and the Veterans Administration for their aid in locating survivors.

The research was greatly facilitated by fellowship support provided by the John Simon Guggenheim Memorial Foundation and the University of California, San Francisco, and a faculty research grant from Mills College.

I also wish to express sincere thanks to Robert Hill, Center for Afro-American Studies, University of California, Los Angeles; Kai Erikson, Department of American Studies, Yale University; Robert Chrisman, publisher and editor, *The Black Scholar*; and Belvie Rooks for their helpful comments on the project.

A special debt of gratitude is owed to professorial colleagues at the University of California, San Francisco: Virginia Olesen, Robert Staples, and Anselm Strauss. As teachers, they demanded work of the highest quality. As colleagues, they were an invaluable intellectual resource. As friends, they were a collective shoulder to lean on.

For help in locating photographs, I am grateful to Yaeko Shinomiya and Eric Cherry of the *Oakland Tribune*, Suzanne Locke of the *San Francisco Examiner*, and Gretchen Rover of the National Liberty Ship Memorial, Inc., San Francisco.

Thanks also to my aunt and uncle, Ruth and Robert Bostick, whose hospitality and good cheer helped me get through sweltering summer weeks of research in Washington, D.C.

Finally, I want to thank my friend and companion, Alice Walker, for her unfailing encouragement and support through sometimes difficult periods of work, struggle, and growth.

—R.L.A.
July 1988

PREFACE

"**R**emember Port Chicago?"

This was the first sentence of a faded pamphlet I had come across one afternoon ten years ago.

No, I didn't remember Port Chicago, although I vaguely recalled reading about antiwar demonstrations during the Vietnam era at a place in California called Port Chicago. But this pamphlet was dated 1945. What had happened in Port Chicago back then?

The pamphlet told of a terrible explosion that occurred there on July 17, 1944. Port Chicago was a naval ammunition base located on the Sacramento River near its entrance into San Francisco Bay, about thirty miles northeast of the city of San Francisco. The gigantic blast instantly killed over three hundred American sailors, totally destroyed two cargo ships that were tied up at the loading pier, wrecked the base itself, and damaged the small town of Port Chicago, located over a mile away. It was the worst home-front disaster of World War II.

Later I was to learn that of the 320 men killed in the explosion some 202 of them were black men who were ammunition loaders. Indeed, every man handling ammunition at Port Chicago was black and every commissioned officer white—this was standard practice in the segregated Navy at that time. On the cover of the pamphlet was a photograph that showed a group of black sailors handling what appeared to be canisters of ammunition, with a huge wall of such canisters rising behind them. Its title was "Mutiny? The real story of how the Navy branded 50 fear-shocked sailors as mutineers."

What mutiny? I read on, ever more curious.

In August 1944, three weeks after the disaster, 328 of the surviving ammunition loaders were sent to load another ship. The men balked, saying they were afraid, and 258 of them were marched off to a barge and held under guard for several days. Eventually, fifty men were singled out, charged with mutiny, court-martialed, convicted, and handed sentences ranging from eight to fifteen years imprisonment.

This all happened in a matter of a few months. By the end of that year the fifty men were in prison at Terminal Island in Southern California. Swift justice indeed. Perhaps too swift.

The burden of the pamphlet's argument was that the accused sailors were not "depraved" men who refused to do their duty, as the prosecution had argued, but young black men, already demoralized by the Navy's policy of racial discrimination, who had been traumatized by the awful explosion in which so many of their friends died. The men were in shock, the pamphlet contended.

And they were hardly grown men. Many were teenagers like John Dunn, a slender seventeen-year-old, or Charles Widemon, nineteen, who signed up at age seventeen, or Martin Bordenave, eighteen, who managed to enlist when he was only sixteen years old.

Then there was Joseph Small, the man labeled by the prosecution as the ringleader of the mutiny. The pamphlet described Small as a clean-cut, intelligent twenty-three-year-old from New Jersey. Small was accused of organizing a "mutinous assembly" of the black seamen.

The prosecutor in the court-martial was a naval officer by the name of James Frank Coakley. That name rang a bell. Wasn't Coakley the DA in Oakland who prosecuted the Black Panthers and antiwar activists in the 1960s?

Not much was said about the defense attorneys, but the pamphlet did mention that Thurgood Marshall had filed a brief on behalf of the fifty men. He charged that the men had been railroaded to prison because of their race. Marshall, now a U.S. Supreme Court justice, was then chief counsel for the National Association for the Advancement of Colored People (NAACP). The pamphlet was, in fact, published by the NAACP Legal Defense and Educational Fund in March 1945, and it included a coupon for making contributions.

I had stumbled across the pamphlet while doing research on the history of blacks in the U.S. Navy for an article I was writing. I laid the pamphlet aside and continued with my work, but I was fascinated by what it reported and I frequently found myself wondering what was the whole Port Chicago story, and what became of the "mutineers."

Turning to my copy of John Hope Franklin's history of black Americans, *From Slavery to Freedom,* I found only a brief mention of Port Chicago. An afternoon at the local library turned up some newspaper and magazine clippings. The explosion was extraordinarily powerful as one of the two ships tied up at the pier was almost fully loaded with thousands of tons of ammunition, bombs, and other explosives. Photos of the base showed a devastated site with timbers, cars, and equipment strewn crazily about. The disaster made the front page of the *New York Times,* but was quickly replaced by other news of the war.

Here and there I found other accounts, but nothing very substantial. Nevertheless, the more I read the more intrigued I became.

There was also a personal resonance which drew me to this story. I was a draft resister during the Vietnam War, thinking that war illegal and racist. I had marched and demonstrated in the 1960s and eventually refused to be inducted into the Armed Forces. Perhaps a bit self-righteously, I felt my stand was the only moral one to take, although I had no enthusiasm for going to jail, the expected outcome. My parents did not oppose my action, but they were troubled by my decision, especially my father. Like me, he was in his twenties when war broke out, but unlike me during the Vietnam War, he was more than willing, if called to duty, to serve the country as a soldier during World War II. He was called—but after a physical examination he was rejected due to a heart condition. A proud man who previously considered himself physically superior—he was an amateur boxer—I think he took that rejection as a personal failure, which was not helped by the fact that several of his brothers served in the war. Within a year he had started on the downward path toward alcoholism.

I tried to explain to my father why I refused to be drafted, but my talk of illegal American intervention in a civil war in Vietnam did not impress him. I think to him, as to many Americans, the Vietnam War was a matter of stopping communism, as World War II had been a matter of stopping fascism. How could I not understand that? He did not accuse me of cowardice or treason; he respected my decision. For me, his attitude toward World War II was something of a puzzle. I connected more with Malcolm X's questioning of black men who allowed themselves to be drafted by white men to fight against colored men.

My father died in 1972, a victim of too much drink. He was fifty-three years old.

I was saved from doing time in jail when a draft case similar to mine came to trial and was thrown out of court on a technicality. The government decided not to prosecute me.

The Vietnam War affected the men of my generation like no other experience. I wish my father could have understood. Surely the gap between us was not unbridgeable.

For his generation World War II was "the good war," a war in which America was clearly on the side of justice, fighting against fascism and racism—or so the school history texts said. Yet, there was often an undercurrent of bitterness in the war stories told by black veterans, anger at some insult or blatant act of discrimination encountered in the military. For black men, World War II was not unqualifiedly a "good war." No doubt my father well knew this, but that did not make him feel better about having been rejected as "unfit." World War II was still the war in which black men proved their mettle in combat for their country.

As I read the Port Chicago pamphlet I couldn't help but think of my father. These were the men of his generation. Many of them were volunteers who, like him, were anxious to prove themselves. Had he been accepted, he might well have wound up at Port Chicago. If he had survived, how would the experience have affected him? Would he have been one of the "mutineers"? Would it have enabled him to understand my action? I couldn't say, but these questions lurked in the back of my mind, and eventually I found an answer of sorts.

Months passed. I was busy with editing, teaching, and various writing projects. I kept a file of Port Chicago clippings and notes, and through the Navy Judge Advocate General's Office I obtained a copy of the transcript of the mutiny trial. I also applied for a Guggenheim Fellowship to do research on the incident. To my delight, a fellowship was offered, which I readily accepted. Perhaps now I could satisfy my curiosity about what happened at Port Chicago.

I soon learned that many records pertaining to World War II had been declassified in 1972 and were now available to researchers. These included records on the Port Chicago explosion and the mutiny case. The documents were available in various repositories including the National Archives, the Library of Congress, the archives of the U.S. Navy Judge Advocate General's Office, the Navy History Library and Operational Archives at the Washington Navy Yard, the Roosevelt Presidential Library in Hyde Park, New York, the Historical Office of the Navy Construction Battalion at Port Hueneme, California, and the San Bruno (Calif.) Federal Records Center. I visited all of them.

I also discovered that there was a book-length account of the Port Chicago incident. Entitled *No Share of Glory* and authored by Robert E. Pearson, this book—now out of print—was published before many of the primary documents were declassified, and I discovered serious factual errors in it. The book also lacked any substantial treatment of how the black enlisted sailors viewed the situation at Port Chicago. The burden of the book, as suggested by its title, was that, because they refused to load ammunition, the black "mutineers" at Port Chicago deserved no share of glory in the defeat of Japan.

As is evident, material from these sources tended to reflect the official Navy point of view about the matter, and to ignore or give little credence to the viewpoint of the black sailors. Consequently, I realized that I must find at least some of the men who had been there if I wanted to get their story.

The task of locating survivors to interview more than thirty-five years after the event proved to be a challenge. From the transcript of the mutiny court-martial I compiled a list of the fifty "mutineers." I began checking this list against telephone directories in the San Francisco Bay Area, where I lived, in hopes that some of the men might have settled there. I found some similar names in the directories, but they were not the individuals I was seeking.

Since the Navy Judge Advocate General's Office had been helpful in furnishing me with a copy of the trial transcript, I took my problem to them. They informed me that any addresses the Navy might have in its personnel files were not available for public use. However, after checking with the Navy's Bureau of Personnel, I learned that if I provided them with a list of the individuals I wished to locate, and prepared a mailing consisting of an unaddressed outer envelope, a cover letter, and a self-addressed return envelope, the Bureau of Personnel would address the envelopes and mail them to the last known address of any individuals from their files who matched those on my list—a so-called blind mailing. I prepared such a mailing for the fifty names and sent it to the Navy Department. Three weeks later I received the first response, from a man living in New York City. Excitedly, I telephoned him and confirmed that he was indeed a Port Chicago survivor who had been involved in the work stoppage and trial. I asked if I might visit him to conduct an interview and he agreed.

Over the next few weeks I received three more responses from the mailing, from survivors who were now living in Washington, D.C., Charleston, South Carolina, and Montgomery, Alabama. All were followed up with telephone calls and requests for interviews.

Meanwhile, I had placed advertisements in several veterans' publications and perused telephone directories from various cities in hopes of locating additional survivors. My efforts were rewarded.

I wrote to U.S. Supreme Court Justice Thurgood Marshall to ask for an interview. He declined, saying he remembered few details from the event. Fortunately, I was later able to track down the NAACP Legal Defense Fund files in a dusty old warehouse in Manhattan, where I found records of the case, including a copy of Marshall's appeal brief and a verbatim transcript of a meeting he had with Navy officials about the case.

With money from the Guggenheim Fellowship I flew to New York, purchased an unlimited-mileage Greyhound bus ticket, and spent two weeks traveling from New York to New Jersey to Washington, and then south to Charleston and Montgomery. I visited the men at their homes and conducted interviews with them. The interviews concentrated on descriptions of their experiences at Port Chicago in the period before the explosion, the explosion itself, and the ensuing work stoppage and court-martial. The interviews were tape-recorded and generally lasted one and one-half to two hours.

Some months later the Veterans Administration also agreed to do a blind mailing for me. Through this mailing I located four additional survivors, one of whom in turn led me to a tenth survivor. Three of these men lived in Los Angeles, two in New York. All agreed to be interviewed.

Meanwhile, the Navy Department informed me that at least twelve of the fifty men were now deceased, and I suspected that others who could not be located were also deceased. Given that the events in question occurred more than three decades ago, and given the high mortality rate among black males, I would not be surprised to learn that most of the fifty men were now dead. I felt fortunate to be able to locate ten survivors, nine of whom I was able to interview. Five of them were among the fifty charged with mutiny; all but one of them, who was seriously injured in the explosion, had taken part in the work stoppage and had personal knowledge of the events leading up to this confrontation.

All of the men told me that I was the first person who had come to ask them about Port Chicago. They were curious about how I had located them and what my purpose was. Indeed, some were more than curious, they were suspicious, thinking that I had some connection with the Navy or the government. Several expressed concern about possible repercussions to themselves or their families as a result of my research. One man was afraid that his son, who worked for the local police department, might be harassed if it were known that his father had been convicted of mutiny. Another refused to accept my assurances of confidentiality and declined to be interviewed after having initially agreed.

I was not without misgivings myself. After the first interview (with a respondent who did not want his son to overhear us because he had never told him about Port Chicago), I wrote an agonizing memo questioning my own motives. What right had I to pry into these men's lives, to expose them and their painful memories to public scrutiny? Was my motive really anything more than curiosity camouflaged as scholarly interest? Having been a draft resister, did I have some axe to grind? Was I not exploiting their suffering in a misguided debate with my dead father? I had no satisfactory answer to these questions, and they haunted me.

But as more interviews took place I came to believe that the interview process was itself therapeutic, both for myself and for the men, who were often relieved to unburden themselves to a sympathetic listener. Moreover, I and my respondents became bonded by a common desire to tell the whole story about what had transpired at Port Chicago. I did not have to offer them any compensation; for most of them, having the opportunity to finally tell their story in full was reward enough.

I found Joe Small by the easiest of all means—I called Information. From the documents, I knew where he was living when he went into the Navy. On the off chance that he had returned to his hometown and still lived there, I called the Information operator in that town. Yes, there was a J.R. Small listed.

I dialed the number. The voice on the other end of the line was gruff and cautious, but he was the man I was looking for. After some explaining, followed by letters, he agreed to be interviewed. I was ecstatic. Here was the man who the prosecution claimed was the ringleader of the mutiny, and he was willing to talk to me. I was pleased but, like Small, I was also cautious, although for different reasons. Would I get the truth from him? Would he tell me the whole story? Would I get a distorted reconstruction, or even an account of things that never happened? I drew up a list of questions for him that would allow me to test the accuracy and completeness of his memory of those events so many years ago—things I could check against the documents I had. No doubt Joe Small also prepared a set of tests for me to pass.

I first met Joe Small at his home on a winter evening in 1977. He was courteous but understandably reserved. I was nervous. Of medium build and height, with alert eyes in a seasoned dark brown face, Joe Small at age fifty-five was a man who made his living by his wits and his hands. He was a house builder and sometime contractor, a "fix-it" man who understood machines. Oddly, the house in which he lived had not been finished. Due to a zoning dispute he was unable to complete the structure. So he and his family lived in what appeared to be the ground floor or basement of an uncompleted house.

We talked, awkwardly enough at first, getting some sense of each other, then feeling more at ease. He introduced me to his wife, Louise, who welcomed me with a warm smile. I pulled out my tape recorder and we talked for an hour or so.

Over the next several years I went back to visit Joe Small a half dozen times. I was going to write a book, I told him at each of our meetings. "I'm sure you will," he replied, but with waning conviction as the years passed.

Yet the work proceeded, sporadically interrupted by teaching, editing, a divorce, part-time fathering, and a midlife crisis. And somehow, fascinating new developments in the story kept popping up to distract me from finishing the book. For a year or so it took off in a surprising new direction—another writer came up with some circumstantial evidence suggesting that the explosion might have been nuclear in origin. Indeed, the atomic bomb that was dropped on Japan a year later was shipped through Port Chicago. Could there have been an earlier shipment, and something went terribly wrong? The evidence was tantalizing, but after many months of searching, nothing hard could be produced to prove the hypothesis and eventually its proponent concluded that it was untenable.

At one point I simply got fed up with the whole project. I felt it was going nowhere. For two years I pretended that I had never heard of Port Chicago. But I couldn't forget it.

Especially could I not forget Joe Small. I had come to respect him and to admire his ability to survive adversity with a sense of humor. To be sure, what he made of it all was not necessarily what I made of it, but the man had heart and an engaging bullheadedness. He was not my father nor, I think, the man my father might have been had he served at Port Chicago. Joe Small was undisputedly himself, but through him, and the other men I interviewed, I came to see the men of my father's generation with new eyes.

The last time I saw Joe Small, in October 1985, he gave me some yellowing typewritten pages. He had written them in the 1960s. In fact, he had shown these to me briefly at the first interview, years before. Like his house (and my project), the manuscript was unfinished. Joe said he didn't think he would finish it, but perhaps I could use it in the book I had been promising to write. The document he gave me was a remarkably vivid account of a day in the life of Port Chicago. I think it had taken him this long to finally decide that I could be trusted with the story—not just these few pages, but the whole Port Chicago story.

With this faded document from Joe Small I came to the end of my research and the beginning of the story.

"To be shot down is bad for the body," said Simple, "but to be Jim Crowed is worse for the spirit."

LANGSTON HUGHES,
"Simple on Military Integration"

Crisis situations . . . are significant objects of sociological inquiry in that they constitute crucibles out of which innovations develop.

TOMATSU SHIBUTANI,
Improvised News

CHAPTER

1

A Day at Port Chicago

M *any years after the war, Joe Small still remembered what it was like being an enlisted man at Port Chicago. He wrote a reminiscence; here is his account:*

This story could start on any day of any week and almost any moment of the day during the years 1943 to 1946. Let's take the 14th day of one of the months in 1944. The day started as usual. The fall-in call came at 6:45 A.M. I never liked powdered eggs so I didn't answer chow call at 5:00 A.M. I also didn't like the white officers—and they were all white—and though I was part of them I didn't like the all-black enlisted-man crew.

The barracks petty officer burst into the overcrowded crew quarters yelling, "Fall out! Fall out, you sons of Satan!" The men who didn't respond quick enough were rolled out of their bunks, mattress and all.

We could hear the clank of metal striking metal outside the barracks window. That would be T.J. He had gotten up at 4:30, stood beside his bunk and used it to relieve his bladder, hung his sneakers around his neck, and gone outside in his skivvies to pitch horseshoes. He had done this every morning for the past two

1

months. We all wondered if he would be successful in getting the Section Eight discharge he was after.

The spring rains had turned the streets of the entire base into a sea of mud, with the exception of the sidewalks around the base officers' quarters. Lieutenant Ernest Delucchi was one of those base officers; in fact, he was the commander of Division Four in Barracks B, my division.

He was a short man in his middle thirties who was making a desperate attempt to change the color of his bars from silver to gold. To get his gold bars he had to prove he could get maximum work out of a crew of black sailors under impossible conditions, and he was doing just that.

Everybody was rushing around talking about last night's liberty, making beds, and listening for the lieutenant's barking voice over the intercom. The petty officer was going from bunk to bunk bouncing a dime on the blankets. If the dime didn't bounce high enough for him to catch it, he ripped the bunk apart and we had to tighten the blanket before we met roll call.

The rains had stopped, the sky was clear of clouds, and it looked like we were in for a nice day. T.J. was dragging around getting his bedclothes together to hang on the fence to dry. He had a date with the medical officer as he had every morning for three weeks. They were running tests on him to find out why he wet his bed every night. His sneakers were still tied together by the laces and hung around his neck. Every time he bent over he had to hold on to them with one hand and then readjust them to keep them from falling off. He mumbled something under his breath about "this stinking bed."

Hoppy, a real black black man, who wore a size 30 suit, stood five feet four inches tall, and weighed 118 pounds soaking wet, crossed the center aisle of the Barn, as we all called the barracks, and said something to T.J. T.J. exploded, hitting Hoppy in the chest with both fists, sending him stumbling backward down the aisle. Hoppy ended up tangled up in two bunks with T.J. screaming at him, "You are just mad because I am getting out and not you!" We all made a break toward the commotion to break up what we thought would be a fight, but there was no need.

Time had run out. It was 6:45. The intercom blasted the louie's voice from the quarterdeck. "Now hear this, now hear this. Division

Four, Barracks B, fall out, fall out!" From that moment we had two minutes to line up in the street, mud or no mud.

I reached after my overshoes to put them on, at the same time my mind was pondering the probable events of the day. There was no reason to believe they would be any different from all the days that had gone before. The shavetail louies always underfoot, the inspectors always yelling to show their authority, the bombs bouncing off the hull of the ship as they rolled down the ramp from the boxcar door across the dock, stopped short of falling into the bay by the ship onto which they would eventually be loaded. And most of all the race. We were always in competition to see which division could load the most ammunition in one eight-hour shift.

A new ship was in and I found myself hoping she had electric winches. We had just sent one to sea with eighteen thousand tons on her. She was drawing about thirty-five feet of water and she was barely gunwale high. One-foot waves flooded her weep holes and put her decks awash. More than one old Liberty had broken in half during a heavy storm under such a load. Her welded seams were rusted, her bulkheads strained out of alignment, her steam lines leaked, and her steam winches looked like they may have been taken off of the steamship that Fulton built. Their valves were leaking and loose, and my hands still bore the blisters of fighting those long iron handles trying to find neutral, which was always in a different place.

The division was lined up in the street, all except me and the POs. I never marched in ranks. It was my job to call cadence for the marching men. The PO stood on the curb waiting for me to call the division to attention. He became impatient and yelled something. I didn't hear what he said but I knew what he meant. I yelled at the top of my voice, "Division, attention!" and waited for the men to pass the word along through a series of yells, elbow jabs, and shoulder shoves. It took a couple of minutes for them to settle down, stop talking, and give me their attention. Then I spoke in a more subdued tone, "Space off to the right." After the "Ready front" the PO called the roster. Every man present answered "Here" after his name was called. Two men that were late returning from liberty somehow had their names answered to.

We saw the cattle car pull up at the end of the street and our DCO came out of the BOQ. I gave the command "Right face, forward march," and began to call cadence. I moved the four lines of men at the rate of sixty-two steps per minute, which was pretty rough in that mud, but that was regulation and the louie was waiting.

The cattle car was our transportation to the docks. It was a forty-foot trailer with a row of small windows along each side about five feet off the floor. It had four rows of benches in it, and fully loaded and packed, it carried about eighty men. It didn't do any good to get in the front of the line to get a seat, because even if you sat for the mile and a quarter ride there was usually someone sitting on your lap, standing on your feet, or standing over you with hands stretched out leaning against the wall. The whole rig was battleship-gray, drawn by a tractor too small for the load.

The doors were closed, locked from the outside by the lieutenant's chauffeur, who jumped back in the lieutenant's jeep and hit his horn twice. The tractor driver started to pull off in first gear. The motor strained, coughed, and died. He started the engine again, this time shifting to low low. He popped the clutch, the truck jumped, picking the front wheels clear off the ground. It piled us all against the rear doors of the cattle car. Hoppy swore at the driver in his deep bass voice. By the time we got straightened out the truck had pulled up in the parking lot, the doors had opened, and the louie was peering into the trailer. "Are you boys okay?" he inquired. I ignored his question, because I knew he was not concerned with our welfare.

I took my usual position to the left and about one third of the way back from the front of the columns of men. A lot of the men were grumbling and cursing. A few were limping. Kong, a short, stocky, gorilla-looking man from Detroit, broke out of ranks and started toward the driver, who had gotten out of the cab and started around the front of the truck. Kong was stopped by the PO and told to get back in ranks. He obeyed after shaking his fists at the driver and promising to see him on the beach.

The DCO of the Third Division was briefing his men on the day's work ahead. They had gotten off a cattle car a few minutes ahead of us and were ready to move out. He made a motion with his finger that brought his PO to stand at attention in front of him. Lowering his voice and looking over his shoulder to see where Lieutenant Delucchi was, he said, "Tom, this hull needs two hundred fifty ton to sail. Tell the boys if we get it by fifteen-thirty, they can hit the beach at eighteen hundred." The PO turned on his heels without answering and walked toward the four columns of men who were talking softly. I didn't hear the command, but I saw all of the men lean forward in anticipation of the command to march, and every left foot started at the same time. Lieutenant Delucchi came around the head of Division Four and met the CO of the Third Division right in front of me. They patted each other on the right shoulder, and Lieutenant Brickland said, "Ernie, you want to kick that another fifty?" My boss said, "Sure." They shook hands very quickly. Lieutenant Brickland moved off up the dock behind his men. Lieutenant Delucchi turned to me and said, "Okay, move them out."

I gave the usual commands and the division moved out. The cadence call came from my lips automatically, but my mind was on the little girl I had met on the beach last night. I don't know whether I picked her up or was picked up by her. Now that I think of it, she really hung one on me.

I didn't like this little town when I first heard about it. It had a soldiers' camp in it, and any sailor would automatically be considered an intruder. Nevertheless, I decided to go. When I got off the bus at this dark corner I didn't know where I was. There was no street sign, not even a streetlight. Everybody went around the front of the bus and turned left, so I just followed the crowd. I was told that in this town sailors stuck together, and everyone that got off the bus had on Navy blues.

I finally reached a little storefront building and peered inside. It had shelves along each wall, and five or six wooden benches in the center of the floor. There was a curtain wall about twenty feet back from the front door. The wall had a door in it with a half-round hole and a shelf at the bottom of the hole. There were five men in the place, all soldiers. A sign over the little window read, "Last Navy Bus Leaves One Thirty A.M." The sounds of talking and laughter were fading away, so I started to trot to catch up. I made mental notes of landmarks in case I had to find my way back alone.

We passed a movie house. The lights lit up the whole street. The marquee stretched all the way to the curb, held up by two enormous chains. The name of the place was the Star. I tried to see what was playing, but my eyes were drawn to the cashier, who sat in a brightly lighted booth in the center of the entrance. She was a beautiful blonde about eighteen or twenty years old. She had a broad smile on her face, but she wasn't smiling at anyone in particular. I think that with the crowd going by, she expected a customer to come to the window.

The sailors were no longer walking in a bunch. The crowd had thinned out and was crossing a street at an angle. On the corner where the leaders were turning right was a large brown stone building. The steeple jutting into the black night sky told me it was a church. There was a light over the door but I didn't see the sign until I started to turn the corner. It was encased in a brick wall about six feet by six feet at an angle to the building. It could be seen from both directions on the street.

According to the sign on the corner, we were walking on Third Street and had just crossed Beach Way. Halfway down the block I could hear water splashing against something, and the smell of fish was very strong. I was used to the smell of salt water, but somehow this smell was different. Then I saw another street sign. This one read, Beach Way and Fourth. I looked back at the sign at the church: someone had turned it around. I thought to myself, kids are the same all over the world.

As we crossed Fourth Street it seemed we had entered a new world, at a different time. The buildings were one-story frame structures, shabbily built, needed paint, and of all things, seemed to be built on poles. The water came right up to the edge of the street, and the houses jutted out into the bay. Though the fronts of the houses rested on the edge of the street, the backs of them were as much as eight feet above the water, supported by poles sticking up out of the sand. All of the buildings I could see were either a saloon, pool hall, chicken shack, or café.

I was thirsty and needed a beer bad. I went into the first saloon I came to. It didn't look bad on the inside. The place was filled with military men, all black except one. At a table at the rear of the room sat two men that were not with the crowd. One black MP and an SP, the only white man in the place.

There was plenty of noise, a jukebox was blasting in the corner, above the laughter and conversation. There seemed to be two women for every man. The most popular thing in any saloon was missing from the bar—beer bottles. The bar, the floor, the tables, and a GI can in the corner were loaded with paper cups. I didn't have to ask why. A broken beer bottle was a perfect weapon in a barroom brawl, and I am sure there were plenty here. I ordered a beer. The bartender set a bottle on the bar but promptly poured it into a paper cup and shoved it to me. The bottle went out of sight behind the bar.

I had passed up the fried eggplant they had for supper at the base, so by this time I was feeling the sting of hunger. A ham sandwich would hit the spot with the beer, but when I asked the bartender for one he said very sarcastically, "We have an agreement with the café across the street. They don't sell beer and we don't serve food." I thanked him, gulped my beer, and headed for the ham sandwich.

I gave the batwing doors of the saloon a vicious push, but they only opened halfway out. I heard a little scream and as I stepped through the opening she was standing there rubbing her right hip. I apologized for the accident. She smiled, and I continued across the street. I looked back over my shoulder wondering what she was doing there, and who she was waiting for. She waved her hand and I imagined I saw a smile. I waved back, stepped through the café door, which was open.

I stopped just inside the door to look for the menu, but I saw none. The sign over the door read "Tender Rib Café." I started toward a long glass counter that had, among other things, a pan stacked high with corn bread. Inside the case were eight or ten glass baking dishes of meat. Though they were all the same color, and all cooked in deep brown gravy, I recognized two of them: the chicken and the pork chops. I looked for the tender ribs, but saw none. There was no ham in sight either; at least if there was, I could not recognize it. I ordered the dish that I thought was chicken—the gravy was a little lighter brown—rice, black-eyed peas, candied yams, and corn bread. I moved across the room, selected a seat, and sat down. There was half a newspaper on the table. I picked it up, it was two days' old. I threw it on a chair against the wall. Just then the waitress called, "Hey, sailor, pick up your plate."

As I leaned forward to get up, she came in the door. I knew she was the girl from across the street by the shorty coat and the pleated skirt she had on. I had never really seen her face. I said to myself, "Damn, she's beautiful!" I picked up my plate from the top of the glass counter and returned to my seat. I began to eat, and suddenly realized I had nothing to drink. Just as I looked up the waitress said, "Coffee, sailor?" I nodded my head and swallowed the mouthful of food I had been chewing. The waitress brought the coffee, cream, and sugar and the bill. The meat didn't taste like any chicken I had ever eaten, so I looked on the bill to see what it was. The bill said, "Dinner $1.90." She had signed her name at the top, Pat.

I was spreading butter on a piece of corn bread when I heard a light giggle. Turning slightly left and looking up, I saw that the girl from across the street had been joined by another girl. I saw something else, everything. That is, had it not been for the green panties under the pleated skirt, I would have seen everything. My jaws stopped moving and I looked up into her face. She was looking directly at me, with a half smile. I tried to let her know what was happening by the movement of my eyes, but she didn't seem to catch the hint. She whispered something to her girlfriend and looked back to me and the smile broadened.

I couldn't eat any more so I stood up, took two dollars and the bill, and laid them on the glass case. I turned and walked straight toward their seats. Her knees were in a normal position and she had a sick look on her face. The other girl was gone.

I said, "Pardon me, miss, I wanted to tell you . . ."

She looked up at me and said, "I don't feel good, will you take me home?" I said sure and reached for her hand. She stood up and said, "My name is Lou." She turned to go to the door.

I put a quarter on the table and picked up her handbag. I waved to the waitress, said, "Good night, Pat," and turned to leave.

Just as I got to the door Pat said, "Good luck, sailor," and waved at me. That put me on my guard and I vowed to be careful.

We had backtracked on Beach Way across Fourth, Third, Second, First, and I wondered what street could be left. We turned right on Front Street, which was well lighted. We hadn't said much to each other, but I did find out that the name Lou was short for Lucinder. That happened when I called her Louise, and she corrected me. I had searched her bag, there was no weapon in it. I had felt her pockets for a knife or maybe brass knucks. There were two other possible places. One I had ruled out; she wouldn't have hidden it there and showed it to me. The other was her hair. I stopped her in her tracks, took her head in both my hands, and kissed her. She didn't resist and there was no weapon.

Just about that time we halted in front of a two-story frame house.

I saw a thin line of light at the edge of one of the front windows, but the porch was dark. As we walked up the steps, I could make out the lines of a porch swing in the shadows. She moved toward the swing, and looking back at me she said, "This is where I live. My mother is waiting up for me." I believed her and ruled out the thought of men waiting in the shadows. If I was going to be robbed it would come as a surprise, because from now on my mind was going on to other conquests.

The footfall of the column leaders on the wooden dock boards brought me back to the present. I called out, "Division halt!" and then, "Fall out!" We were at work and I was tired already.

I heard the clang of metal against metal and looked up. There she was, riding high in the bay. A brand-new Liberty. I knew she must be electric all the way. I bet she hadn't been out of Kaiser Ship Yards long enough to roster her full complement of merchantmen. The graveyard shift was just getting off. I asked the PO, "How much did you get?" He spoke out of the corner of his mouth, "A hundred ninety, and is he mad."

I stepped around five one-ton bombs in a huge wire net and headed for the gangplank. I was almost eager to get to those beautiful electric winches, running them was a breeze. I walked up between the two control panels. Each had a handle about six inches long about belt high, and comfortable to the grip. I stood on a rubber mat right at the edge of the hold. I could see all the way to the bottom of the ship. She had three decks, and the bottom of the hold was about fifty feet down.

Hoppy was my signalman for today. He stood at the edge of the hold talking with Kong. The hook was in the bottom well of the hold so there was nothing for him to do until we started the first lift from the dock. The net still had two other bombs on it, and the crew was slowly making their way down the series of ladders that were welded to the steel hull of the ship. Kong yelled my name and started toward me on shaky legs, looking more like a tamed gorilla than a human. He said, "Man, I got loaded last night."

"That I can see and so did Lieutenant Delucchi," I said.

"Oh, damn Tubby!" Kong said. "He got pretty tanked up himself last night. He staggered in the same time I did this morning. I want to tell you about this broad I met last night. But then it wasn't a broad after all. I met her in the J Bar on Seventh Street. I spent over twenty bucks on her. Man, was she fine! Anyhow we got to this room about two-fifteen this morning. Man, was I ready for Freddie!

"I noticed she didn't turn on the lights when we went in, but I didn't care, there was enough light from the Navy Yard across the street for me to see what was in the room. I could see the bed and I headed straight for it. The light went off under the bathroom door, it opened, and something flew across the room and landed half on, half off the chair. The shadow that passed between me and the window was wrong. There was a few things missing. The long hair, the full bust, and the wide hips. Man, did I flip!

"Instead of coming around the bed, it got lost in the shadows against the wall. I heard the key rattle in the door, the tumblers fell over, and the key came sliding toward me across the floor. It went under the bed."

I asked him, "Why didn't you get out of there?"

He said, "Man, I had taken off my pants, shoes, and hat, and didn't know where they were! I rolled out of bed and went to the bathroom. There was the hips, the bust, and the long hair all piled up in the bathtub. There was a funny-looking object lying on the sink. I picked it up to examine it. It was a straight-edge razor blade that slid back in a metal handle. When you compressed the button it slid forward exposing the blade and locked in place. I pulled the bathroom door open and headed across the room to the switch by the door. I flipped the switch, the light came on. I heard a scuffle and whirled around. The punk was headed for the bathroom, but he was late on the move, I had his knife."

Hoppy cut in in an excited voice, "Man, what did you do?"

Kong continued, "Without looking around, I made a dive for my pants that were on the floor at the foot of the bed. By the time I got them on he was headed toward me naked, at a dead run. He reminded me of a goat on a charge. He was running in a crouch with his head down."

Waves began running up the cable from the hold. That told me the net was ready. I looked over in the hold, pulled back on the inboard control three clicks, and told Kong he better get to work. I took up four clicks on the outboard line and waited for the net to come into view above the edge of the hold. Hoppy moved over to his position at the rail to await the descent of the net. All movement and safety of equipment, material, and personnel depended on his signals from the time the net dropped below the rail until the time it came back into my field of vision. He was standing facing me and looking over the rail at the men loading the nets. By holding his hand in front of him and clinching his left fist, he stopped the net six inches above the dock. The men pushed the net to the side about ten inches off center. By holding his hand out in front of him, pointing his left index finger downward, and moving it in a circular motion, Hoppy gave me the signal to lower the outboard line. I pushed the outboard winch control two clicks forward and dropped the net on the dock.

A clinch of his left fist told me the hook was low enough for the men to unhook the empty net and hook up the loaded one. The hook swung back to center, across center, and stopped, hanging at an angle. A loud handclap from Hoppy brought my eyes back to his hands. Rubbing his palms together slowly meant slow movement; the left index finger pointed upward meant up on the outboard line. I pulled the outboard winch control back one click, never taking my eyes off his hands. Moving his finger a little faster meant more power. I added one more click to the winch. I could hear the net dragging down the dock until it came back to center directly below the outboard boom. The clinching of his left fist stopped all motion. I pushed the control back to neutral. Hoppy brought the tips of his fingers together on each hand and then brought his two hands together in a backward and forward motion, first touching his fingers together and then parting them, followed by touching them together again. This meant fast movement. The left index finger pointed upward and moving fast, and the right index finger pointed upward and moving slowly, gave me my orders. I pulled four clicks on the loaded line and two clicks on the slack line. I had to watch both Hoppy and the line—him to catch any signal for an emergency stop, and the line to see the load when it cleared the rails.

As the loaded net rose above the rails, I added two more clicks to the slack line and backed off two on the loaded line. As the inboard line became taut and started to draw the net in over the rail of the ship, I let it pull until the net got high enough to clear the edge of the hold. As the net crossed between us we had to inspect the net and the load that was in it. If a bomb fell out or the net came loose and dumped the load into the hold, it would mean disaster. There is absolutely no place to run or hide in the hold of a Liberty ship being loaded with ammunition.

The load and net seemed to be fine, but as the side of the hold came into my field of vision, I saw something. Hoppy saw him the same time I did. He yelled, "Hot!" at the top of his voice. I had to act almost without thinking. I stopped the inboard winch and reversed the outboard winch full speed. That took the net and load almost straight up. The load was about twelve inches above the deck before I got a chance to stop it and look down. A 90-Day Wonder [new officer] was kneeling at the edge of the hold. I let off the inboard line, the net began to shift back toward the rail of the ship. When it was far enough away from the edge of the hold, I let off the outboard winch and landed the net load of bombs on the deck of the ship.

Lieutenant Delucchi came running. I expected him, because under the strain of five tons of bombs and both winches running under load, the springs started to sing, and he heard it. This holdup meant a loss of tonnage to him and he was hot as a pepper mill. The shavetail lieutenant had a bloody mouth that he received when the net hit him and he bumped it on the side of the hold. He was lucky. If the net had been two inches lower he would have gotten knocked into the hold. The lines and springs were inspected and found to be unbroken. The shavetail was led away and we returned to work. Lieutenant Delucchi came over, patted me on the shoulder, and said, "Make it up, Randy. We need three hundred tons."

The twenty-fifth load was headed up when the ship's bells tolled 1200 hours. I dropped the load back on the dock and went to chow. We were five lifts—or twenty-five tons—behind. I knew we had to make it up before 1530 hours or face the maddest Italian in the Navy.

The chow wagon had arrived, manned by two cooks and three KPs. The men were lined up in single file, all jabbering about one thing or another. I fell in behind Hoppy, goosed him with my knee, and looked around to see if one of the marine guards had seen me. Hoppy yelled and grabbed the sailor in front of him in a bear hug. He immediately began to say "I'm sorry" over and over and to point back over his shoulder at me. The sailor laughed and said forget it. We picked up our trays from the ammo box at the side of the truck and gripped it firmly in both hands. Experience had taught us that the KPs always seem to enjoy serving chow, because that's when they get even with the Navy by trying to knock the bottom out of the trays with their serving spoons.

The fare was liver and onions, or bacon. I got bacon. Though I was raised on a farm and grew up eating onions, I quit when a girl refused to kiss me one night because I had onions on my breath. It turned out I didn't need kisses to fire up her boilers anyhow. It was a good thing the Navy used stainless-steel trays, as the KP tried to poke his fork through the bottom of it. After that, it was safe to turn one side of the tray aloose with one hand.

I picked up two pieces of hand-sliced bread and a cup of coffee, and looked around for a place to sit. Hoppy and Kong were saving me a seat on a rope dock bumper at the edge of the water. I set my mug down on what used to be an 8-by-8-inch dock edge guard. Now it was about 8 by 4 half round. Kong spotted the driver who had given us the rough time coming to work, now sunning himself in the parking area, and started to get up. I put my hand on his shoulder and said, "The beach is better." Kong said, "Yeah," and stuffed a piece of liver in his mouth.

One of the KPs was headed toward us with a handful of liver and an apple pie. He said, "You guys missed your pie. They were getting some more when you went by." We each got two slices of pie and a piece of liver and the KP turned to go back to the chow wagon. He stopped short and turned around and said, "You guys from 4B?" We all answered yes at the same time. Then he asked, did we hear about T.J.? None of us answered, we all stood up. He continued, "We heard they gave him some sort of shock treatment in sick bay, and he went blind. They took him to the hospital across the bay." Hoppy said that ends the pissy smell in the barn. I said maybe he will get a medical instead of S.8. Kong said he ought to get a BCD for stinking up the barracks.

We picked up our trays and headed for the GI can at the rear of the truck. The marine on guard looked over each tray carefully, to make sure there was no food being thrown away. You took all you wanted, and you ate all you took. The truck was all closed up and loaded except for the GI can, the trays, and eating tools. The cooks were already screaming, "Let's roll 'em!" They had been on duty since 4:00 A.M. and their day was finished after serving second chow. The cooks who came on at 1200 served third chow at 1700 hours. The night shift served first chow at 0530.

Lieutenant Delucchi was getting out of his jeep. He had driven himself to the BOQ for lunch. I had discussed with him many times the possibility of an explosion on the dock, but he always laughed it off. I told Hoppy and Kong to go aboard and I waited to talk to him. He walked up alongside of me, looked at his watch, and asked, "How are things going?"

"Rough, I think we are pushing too hard," I said.

He looked at his watch again and asked, "Do you think you can lift thirty by fifteen-thirty?"

"Sure, if the place doesn't blow up, and someday it will."

"If it does," he said, "neither you nor I will be around to know about it," and broke out with one of his belly laughs.

That made me mad, so I quickened my step and mounted the gangway at a dead run.

Hoppy wasn't at his post so I couldn't go right to work. I thought about Lou. I could have had her right there on the swing, at least I thought so. But maybe that was my ego talking. She somehow didn't act like that sort of girl. I had walked many hookers to their bed or bunk, and by this time they had told me how much and showed me a health card.

The inside door opened and a small-built woman in a beautiful floor-length pink housecoat asked, "Is that you, Lucinder?"

The girl moved across the swing and answered, "Yes, Momma."

Just as the light flicked on and the screen door opened, I stood up. The lady said, almost in a whisper, "Oh, you have a friend with you. Come in, both of you."

I looked at my watch. It was 11:30. I said, "No, thank you. I think I will be heading back."

Lou took me by the arm and gave it a little tug. Her mother said, "Not on your life! This is Lucinder's first night home and she has met a friend already. Come in, young man, come in."

Lou had slid her arm around my waist as if to keep me from running away. She squeezed gently, and when I looked down at her she smiled, touched two fingers to her lips, and then touched them to mine. I placed my arm on her shoulder and my fingers touched her breast. I squeezed the nipple, expecting a lightning swing from her right hand. Instead, she let out a little squeal and laid her head on my shoulder. I had to change my thoughts immediately. Those tight sailor pants would have given me away when we entered the living room. It was very brightly lit, and there was the distinct odor of new paint.

I saw Hoppy coming up the gangway taking three steps at a time. The winches whirred into action, and we were off and running.

My first lift off the dock I noticed the winch pulled a little too hard. I paid close attention to the drums to see if the lines were fouled or bedded. When the load started to cross the deck, I could see why the springs were tight and the winches dragged. There was an extra bomb in the net. We were lifting six tons instead of the regular five. The POs were really trying to get that extra twenty-five tons.

The ship on the other side of the dock was almost loaded. She was getting ready to sail. I could hear the crew battening down the hatches. She would probably sail with the tide tomorrow morning. I found myself hoping she made it across. The Atlantic was thick with Germans and the Pacific was overcrowded with Japs. If God smiled on her and the Japs and Germans missed her, there were still the storms and the high seas. We had just gotten the report that half a Liberty had been towed in. She broke in half, in twenty-two-foot seas, and the stern half went down. They didn't tell us how many men were lost but we all knew the crew's quarters were in the fantail. If those boxcars weren't there, I could see if the rats were leaving the ship. That was a sure sign there would be trouble on the trip.

I dropped a load in the hold, and instead of setting it down, the PO stopped it about six inches short of the deck. The crew swung the net to one side and I lowered it gently to the deck. Instead of waiting for the crew to unload the net, I was waved out of the hold. I soon found out why. Lieutenant Delucchi had added another net. There was no more resting between lifts. There was always a net loaded and ready to go aboard, and always one empty and ready to be lifted out of the hold. The DC was going to win his fifty or burn up the winches and kill the crew.

The bombs hitting the ship and the dock edge guard became louder and more frequent. The cursing and swearing were more constant. A few fights erupted, but the crew chief was there to quiet things down. I had no time to gab with Hoppy or anyone else now. I paid close attention to my winches, for I expected the brakes to start heating at any time. After all, I was lifting six tons at a clip and, what was worse, stopping six tons in almost free-fall. I could usually smell the brake bands before they started smoking. But if the wind was blowing the wrong way, I might not see or smell the hot bands until it was too late. That would be when I had to make an emergency stop because of someone in the drift path, or someone standing under a descending load that I couldn't see until after the load started to descend.

I noticed civilians coming down the dock. Each carried a flight bag, a small suitcase, or a duffel bag. They had to be the crew of the ship in the next berth. They all swaggered in their walk as if the screws that held their knees together were loose. Learning to keep your balance while walking on a moving floor causes sea legs after a few years, and when you walk on land you swagger at the shoulders and often appear to be slightly drunk. When I noticed the smoke billowing from the ship's funnels I knew she was getting up steam. She would convert the steam to energy that would carry her on a journey not yet known, to encounter she knew not what. But go she must, for men were waiting on what she was carrying to kill other men who were waiting on other ships to do the same.

The appearance of the jitney to switch boxcars meant a ten-minute break. I was glad, it would give my winches a few minutes to cool down. Kong came up the gangway with a canteen in his hand. He grabbed Hoppy by the shoulder and continued to where I was sitting between the two winches. Hoppy sat on the edge of the hold. Kong jumped up on the winch brake drum but immediately jumped down—it was hot. I asked him what was in the canteen. Kong opened his mouth to say something, but Hoppy grabbed it and opened it. At the same time he said, "What happened to that punk last night?"

Kong rubbed his buttocks and said in an excited voice, "What happened to the punk? Man, what about me? That was the strongest man I ever tangled with. I ducked that first charge and he ran into the wall. While he was getting himself together and untangled from the clothes tree he ran into, I dragged the bed away from the wall to find the key. I found it but before I could get it in my pocket he was all over me. We wrestled for a while and he got a bear hug on me. Man, I couldn't move! He was squeezing the breath right out of me. I tried to butt him in the face with the back of my head. I tried to break his ribs with my elbow. He kept calling me a son of a bitch and squeezing harder. I finally got a handful of his privates and then I did some squeezing. He bit me on the shoulder and then started to weaken. He released his hold enough for me to break free. He called me a motherfucker several times and started slipping to the floor. I gave his balls a squeeze as hard as I could and let go. He slumped to the floor out cold.

"I thought I had plenty of time so I got dressed and started for the door. Then I thought about his money, he must have had some somewhere. I found his handbag but there was absolutely nothing in it. Man, I mean it was empty! There wasn't even a pin in it!"

"I know that guy had some aching nuts this morning," Hoppy said.

"His nuts! My ribs feel like they need cementing back together."

"Did you find any money?" I asked him. "They always keep a bundle somewhere."

"Let me tell you, you won't believe this. I found the money, three hundred dollars. It was in the pocket of a pair of dungaree shorts in the bottom of a grocery bag he used as a clothes hamper in the bathroom."

Hoppy jumped up. He said, "Man, you been holding out on us! When we hit the beach tonight the juice will be on you!"

"I ain't got the money," Kong said.

"What happened?" I asked.

"If I had squeezed a gorilla's nuts that hard he would have stayed out for a week. But when I opened the door he was getting up off the floor. I tried to get past him to the door. I made it but the damn door was locked. I had to take the money out of my pocket to get the key. By that time he was on his feet and headed for me. I got the key in the door and unlocked it, but I didn't have time to open it. He came at me with his head down just like before. All of a sudden he fell flat on the floor and came at me sliding on his stomach. He grabbed my legs and upset me. I fell back against the door and knocked the light out. I jumped up and opened the door. I could see him getting up, so I turned on the fan. He followed me out into the hall buck naked."

I asked again, "What happened to the money?"

"I dropped it when he hit me. It was three one-hundred-dollar bills. Anyway, I lost him when I crawled through a hole in the Navy Yard fence across the street."

Two short toots from the jitney whistle, asking for a clear track off the dock, let us know it was time to go back to work. It would take the dock crew about five minutes to open the doors and set the skids, so I decided to get a drink of water.

Darn the girl! Every time she finds my mind unattended she moves in. I remember hurrying across the room to a deep stuffed chair and sitting down. Lou's mother skirted around canvas-covered furniture in the dining room and into the kitchen. The pivot door swung back and forth four or five times and then there was silence. The light I expected to come on never did. The offer to have coffee I expected never came. Lou had put on some records and turned out some lights. As she crossed the room and sat on the arm of the chair beside me, Mahalia Jackson was singing "He's Got the Whole World in His Hands."

"Where is your mother?" I asked.

"Don't worry about her. She likes and trusts you or she would be sitting right there. She's gone to bed."

I thought that was my cue. I pulled her down on my lap, but she swung around and stood up. I stood up with her. I pulled her to me and kissed her hard and long. When I let her go she drew a deep breath and said, "Honey, don't rush me. I don't even know if you are married or not."

She backed away, straightening her skirt. I noticed the rapid rise and fall of her breasts and surmised that that kiss had really started the fire. I couldn't let it die now. I pulled her up to me and asked her, "Why the display in the café?"

She looked up at me and said, "I'm sorry. That was a mistake. I didn't mean to tempt you. I am ashamed of how it looked to you." She stopped short and looked straight at me. She asked, "What is your name?"

This stopped me cold, so I covered up the moment for thought by squeezing her nipple. She never blinked an eye. I pulled her up to me and kissed her. Then I told her, "I have several names. I have one when I wear civvies and another when I am a sailor, so tonight my name is Randolph."

The bombs started crashing against the ship. I went back to my winches. Delucchi got his tonnage and his fifty dollars and it was quitting time. The cattle car was back; the night crew was unloading and we were forming ranks to march off the dock. I was in my place at the side of the column about to yell "Forward, march" when the louie tapped me on the shoulder. He had the tally sheet in his hand. He put his arm around my shoulder and with a big smile said, "Thanks, Randy. You did a fine job. We got five ton over." I said, "And fifty dollars." He turned a pale green, gave a grunt like a pig, and walked off toward the cattle wagon.

As the cattle car wound its way through the ammo bunkers over the bumpy road, its motor screaming and Hoppy cursing the driver, my mind pondered the possibility of the whole place blowing up. True, the bombs had no detonators in them, and as far as the Navy was concerned, it couldn't happen, but those bombs were full of gunpowder and the way they were handled anything *could* happen. I found myself hoping that if and when it did, I would be miles away from there.

Someone mentioned T.J.'s name and I cocked my head to listen. All I could hear was that he got a bad conduct discharge. I started forcing my way to the door. My mind was in a whirl and I had to get the straight of this. After all, if the man was blind, how could they give him a BCD? When the door opened I was the first one to hit the sod. I didn't wait to march the men off, I headed for the supply room. That punk that ran it would have the complete story on everything. I mounted the steps two at a time and threw my weight against the door. It squeaked and swung open. There was no one behind the counter. I yelled as loud as I could, "Tony, where are you?" Tony answered from the back room, "Be right there." I picked up a couple pair of socks and stuffed them in my pocket, hoping they were the right size, and had just got my fatigue jacket down when Tony came out, brushing his straight black hair with his hand. I asked him, "Man, what happened to T.J.?" Tony started cracking up. That made me feel better. His laughter seemed to take the importance out of what I had heard. I knew then that it must have been a lie.

"T.J. is in the brig. He went to the hospital for examination after someone told the doctor that he saw T.J. wetting in his bed after he had gotten out of it. The shock treatment was a fake. They thought it would scare him into giving up his schemes to get out. When he pretended to go blind . . ."

"Pretended?" I said.

"Sure, there never was anything wrong with him. When he claimed he couldn't see he really shook up them doctors. He even threatened to sue the whole damn bunch. They thought maybe he had taken some kind of drugs and sent an MP to search his locker."

Just then the back door opened and closed again but no one came in. It was almost chow time so I said to Tony, "They found dope?"

"No. They found a book about a woman who was in a car accident and sued because of an injured back. She won the case because they couldn't prove her back wasn't injured."

I started laughing and pounding on the counter. I said, "So he tried it with his eyes?"

"Yes, but you haven't heard the best yet," Tony said. "They thought he was faking, so they got one of the female nurses to take off everything except her bra and panties and walk through the room he was in."

"And the fool got a hard-on," I said.

"They couldn't tell. He had his sneakers on his lap, but they took movies of him. Once the nurse got in front of him, his eyes followed her all the way across the room and out the other door. He's still trying to fake it. . . ."

Here the story breaks off and poor T.J.'s fate remains unrecorded. Joe Small, "Randy" in this account, never completed the story— though he lived it through to the finish.

After talking with Joe Small and others who were there, and reading the records, I seek to complete the telling of their story.

CHAPTER

2

The Day—
July 17, 1944

To Seaman First Class Joseph Randolph Small it looked like it would be another ordinary day at Port Chicago, a day of hard work relieved only by the men's banter and joking. Nothing to write home about, but then there seldom was.

Small climbed out of his upper bunk bed, dressed quickly, and then roused the other men in the barracks, as he usually did. The barracks was soon alive with the talking and laughter of a hundred or so young seamen. With clear brown skin, broad shoulders, and a slight moustache, Joe Small, who stood five feet seven inches tall, was sturdily built. At almost twenty-three years of age he was one of the older enlisted men, and some of the younger men looked up to him like an older brother. They certainly respected him more than they did the petty officers, who were considered brownnosers and "slave drivers." Small could be counted on to stand up for the men, and he in turn enjoyed their respect. It was one of the few rewards to be had at Port Chicago. Even the officers recognized and to some extent sanctioned Small's special standing with the enlisted men, signalized by the fact that it was Small who was customarily assigned to march outside of ranks and call cadence.

Had he been older, his commanding officer once told him, he might have been considered for advancement to petty officer.

Of course there were also occasional run-ins with petty officers (usually black) and the commissioned officers (always white), but Small generally came out unscathed. He had been at Port Chicago for the better part of a year now and he knew the ropes. He wasn't afraid of the officers like some of the younger guys, although he respected the officers' power. In another time and circumstance Joe Small knew he could have been an officer himself, but this was Port Chicago in 1944.

At Port Chicago the Sacramento River widens into a bay—the Suisun Bay—that is a few miles across at its widest point. Port Chicago lies on the south bank of the river, and in the middle of the river, just north of Port Chicago, is a string of islands; at night a light shone from the lighthouse on the nearest island, Roe Island. Low, rolling hills paralleled the course of the river, forming a flat plain between the river and the hills. On this plain war-related industries, such as aviation fuel refineries, steel mills, and chemical plants, sprang up along with purely military installations: the huge Army staging area at Camp Stoneman in the town of Pittsburg upstream from Port Chicago; the Army arsenal at Benicia and the huge Navy shipyard at Mare Island downstream. Farther yet, beyond the hills toward the west, were Oakland and San Francisco —and more enormous military installations. The San Francisco Bay Area was one great center from which men, weapons, and matériel were poured into the Pacific war.

The ammunition depot at Port Chicago was one of the main sources of supply for the Pacific fleet. The dock facilities could handle the largest ammunition carriers in the Navy. The base was built around a road shaped like a "Y," with the upper arms ending at the river. At the end of the right arm was a 1,200-foot wooden pier curving out into the river. Upriver a short distance was a new, longer marginal pier still under construction. Downriver about a mile, just on the other side of the left arm of the "Y," were a dozen or so buildings, including the two-story barracks buildings occupied by the black enlisted seamen. Between the arms of the "Y" and to the right of it were about forty barricaded revetments in each of which a half dozen or so railroad boxcars loaded with ammunition could be stored. (For safety reasons, the boxcars were kept in the revetments until immediately before they were rolled onto the pier to have their explosive contents transferred to ships.) At the bottom of the "Y" were the headquarters buildings and officers' quarters. Where the "Y" ended, the base road intersected with a county road leading into the town of Port Chicago, a mile and a half distant from the loading pier. With a few hundred homes and businesses the town was quite small, and the white townspeople watched somewhat uneasily as the mainly black Navy base grew rapidly to rival the town in size.

The men of the Fourth Division marched to the mess hall for breakfast. Afterward they were loaded onto trailers, dubbed "cattle cars" by the men, for the short drive to the ships' pier and the beginning of their workday at 8:00 A.M. Their work was to load ammunition, bombs, and other high explosives from railroad box-cars into the holds of waiting cargo ships. The work was hard and dangerous—but it had to be done. The war effort depended on it.

The Port Chicago seamen didn't know it, but their labors had contributed materially to the success of the Allied push in the Pacific. With superior firepower Allied units were advancing in the Marianas and New Guinea, and the Japanese were losing ground. In Europe the Allies were reclaiming France and Italy, while the Russians were pressing the Germans on the eastern front. Retreating Nazi units in Russia stopped just long enough to desecrate the grave of Alexander Pushkin, the great black poet revered by the Russian people.

For the most part the Port Chicago men were good workers. Certainly there was the occasional slacker, but most of the men worked hard, and they got the tonnage loaded time and time again. In fact, the Fourth Division was considered about tops among the loading divisions at the base.

The hard labor and physical danger were real, but men learned to accommodate themselves to these ever-present companions. Less tolerable to some of the men was the thing that was immediately apparent to any new arrival from boot camp: all of the men actually physically handling the ammunition boxes and bombs were black, and all of the commissioned officers, marine guards, and civilian skilled workers were white. It was a Jim Crow base. Not that racial segregation was unexpected—although in 1944 there was growing and vocal opposition to the practice among blacks and white liberals—but it assuredly was not a boost to the morale of the enlisted men.

On this day Small and the other men of the division were to finish loading the S.S. *Mormactern*. The *Mormactern* had been loading at the pier since July 12, and was to sail in the early afternoon of the 17th. Arriving at the pier, the men quickly grouped themselves into squads at each of the ship's five holds and on the pier. Liberty awaited them at the end of eight hours of toil.

At 8:30 A.M. Lieutenant Paul G. Zacher arrived at Port Chicago from his home in Oakland. Zacher was assigned to Port Chicago as a loading officer out of the port director's office. As loading officer his duties included inspecting vessels, keeping track of the plan of stowage of the ammunition aboard each vessel, and seeing to it that various loading regulations were followed.

It was a busy time for Zacher. Just the day before, he had gone to Martinez, farther down the river, to inspect the S.S. *Quinalt Victory* at the Shell Oil Company dock. The *Quinalt Victory* was a new vessel of the Victory type owned by the U.S. Government's War Shipping Administration and operated for the government by the United States Line Company. The ship had been delivered by its builders only a week before, on July 11. After a few days of tests by the new crew the *Quinalt Victory* sailed from Portland to San Francisco, passing through the Golden Gate on the morning of July 16. Steaming north past Alcatraz Island, the vessel pushed on into the treacherous narrows of the Carquinez Straits, through which the Sacramento emptied into the great bay. Spanned by a spindly bridge, the straits were bordered on the north by the town of Vallejo and the huge Mare Island naval shipyard. Along the Sacramento flowed a constant stream of men and war supplies.

The *Quinalt Victory* was soon to start loading at Port Chicago, but first it docked at Martinez, another of the many river ports. The stopover here was to take on a load of fuel oil. While the ship was being fueled Lieutenant Zacher came aboard to make his inspection. The vessel was clean, as he expected, being just out of the shipyard. Most of the booms were in their cradles and a deck crew was putting the preventer guys in place. It appeared to Zacher that as soon as the fueling was finished the ship would be ready for loading. He instructed the chief mate to have all gear in place ready to start.

That was the day before. Today Zacher knew the *Quinalt Victory* was due to arrive momentarily at Port Chicago—which meant that the *Mormactern* had to complete loading and depart to clear a berthing space at the pier. Fortunately, when he got to the ships' pier it was evident that the work was on schedule. Loading should be finished by noon. The *Mormactern* had taken on almost 3,500 tons of ammunition. Finishing up should present no problems.

Zacher could now turn his attention to the S.S. *E. A. Bryan*, which rode deep in the water on the inboard, landward side of the pier. The *Bryan* had docked on the morning of July 13 and Zacher had been aboard the vessel every day since, checking the loading. The situation seemed to be normal; most days he noted nothing unusual. By the morning of the 17th the *Bryan* was loaded with some 4,200 tons of ammunition and bombs. The *Bryan* was scheduled to take on 8,500 tons.

The *Bryan* was a vessel of the Liberty type owned by the War Shipping Administration and operated by the Oliver J. Olson Company. Designed as an "emergency" addition to U.S. maritime shipping capability during the war, Liberty ships (and the somewhat better equipped Victory ships) could be built quickly and cheaply. Called "the ships that were built by the mile and chopped off by the yard," some 2,710 Liberty ships were built and put to sea between 1941 and 1945. (A few still ply the seas as tramp freighters, and the last pristine example, the *Jeremiah O'Brien*, is anchored at Fort Mason in San Francisco.) The typical Liberty ship had five cargo holds, three in the forward section of the ship and two aft. Each hold was as deep as a four-story building. Three masts supported loading booms, with the bridge superstructure and smokestack in the middle of the ship. Just over 440 feet long, a Liberty ship carried a crew of fifty-two men and a gun crew of twenty-nine. Capable of making only eleven knots, Liberty ships were slow but dependable.

Put in service in February 1944, the *Bryan* had made one transpacific trip. After some minor voyage repairs the vessel was deemed fit and sent to Port Chicago to load for another trip. Since the morning of the 13th the ship had been loading continuously, around the clock.

Shortly after noon, Zacher and Lieutenant Norman Erlandson stood on the dock and watched as a squad of enlisted men unloaded boxes of detonating fuses from a railroad boxcar. The men swung the boxes from the car doorway onto a wooden board surrounded by a wire net. They were pushing hard to get the job finished, so that the boxes stacked on the board could be hoisted into the ship's hold. By 1:15 P.M. the *Mormactern* would be leaving the pier, much to the relief of Lieutenant Zacher.

For the most part the loading of the *Bryan* had been proceeding routinely, but not without problems. There had been trouble with the steam winches. The winches were manually operated and were used to hoist loads of cargo from the pier into the ship's holds. A winch was located at each of the five cargo holds. Most of the trouble was with bearings and valves.

The very day the *Bryan* arrived at Port Chicago and began loading there was trouble with the No. 1 winch. The third mate, Herman Jacobsen, was told that the brake on the winch was stuck. It was stuck in the "off" position, which meant that the winch operated freely, and so long as there was adequate steam pressure its movements could be controlled even without the use of the brake. Jacobsen's view of the problem was expressed when he later testified that "the brake is something that a real winchman never uses, and naturally gets stiff."

However, if steam pressure were suddenly lost while a load was being hoisted, only a functioning brake could prevent the load from dropping violently onto the pier or into the ship's hold, with possibly disastrous consequences. Jacobsen called the chief mate and the chief engineer, who came up and looked at the winch, but it was unclear whether the brake was ever repaired. To Jacobsen's knowledge nothing was done about the brake, but not being an engineer, he didn't inspect it. In any event he received no further complaints from the winch operators about it. Brake or no brake, the winchmen had their orders and a job to do.

More problems occurred on the night of Saturday the 15th when the crank bearing on the No. 2 winch began making a hammering noise. The oiler, William Hampton, kept greasing it, and the next day the chief engineer and the deck engineer replaced the failing bearing.

Later, on the afternoon of July 17, a bleeder valve on the No. 4 winch had gone out and had to be repaired. Albert Carr, a civil service plumber from Pittsburg, California, was called in to fix it. Carr came aboard the *Bryan* at about 3:00 P.M.; it was his first day working at Port Chicago. The nipple on the bleeder valve was broken. Carr removed the broken part, went to the shop at the pier and got a new nipple and new valve, and installed them. "That was all the labor that I done," he would say later.

After Carr finished, the ship's engineer operated the winch to check it. As the engineer manipulated the winch Carr began to edge away.

"Where are you going?" the engineer asked.

"Well, I am through. That's all right, isn't it?" Carr was feeling nervous. "I don't like the looks of things around here," he told the engineer. Carr didn't like the looks of all the shells and explosives he saw on the pier. He wasn't used to it. He turned and watched some enlisted men as they rolled bombs down a ramp from a boxcar. Men were on each side of the ramp holding on to the heavy bombs. As Carr looked on, one man lost his grip on a shell; it dropped two feet and hit the deck with a thud. Nothing happened, but Carr was ready to get away from the pier.

Shortly after 5:00 P.M. Lieutenant Zacher spoke with Lieutenant John Christenbury, loading officer of the *Bryan*. The ninety-eight men of the Third Division were now at work on the *Bryan*. They were loading boxes of 5"/38 projectiles into the No. 1 hold. Depth bombs were being loaded into the No. 2 hold, and 5,000-pound bombs into the No. 3 hold. Holds No. 4 and No. 5 were being loaded with twenty- and forty-millimeter shells. Zacher saw nothing unusual in the moments before he left the pier. There was no reason to think the *Bryan* would not be loaded and ready to go to Richmond for a deck load on July 22 as planned. At 5:20 Lieutenant Zacher completed his duties and left the base.

The *Quinalt Victory* still had not arrived; it would not dock at the pier until 6:00 P.M. After it docked some 102 men of the Sixth Division, many of them only recently arrived at Port Chicago, would be assigned to rig the ship in preparation for loading. Loading of ammunition onto the *Quinalt Victory* was scheduled to begin at midnight.

3
Black Men and the U.S. Navy

L ike many of the men working at Port Chicago, Joe Small's presence there was largely accidental. Born on September 1, 1921, in Savannah, Georgia, Small spent most of his youth on truck farms in New Jersey, where his family moved in 1927. His father, Albert W. Small, was a farmer and part-time Baptist preacher; Annie Eliza Small, his mother, cared for the house and his three brothers and one sister. Small's father died in 1936, and the family got through the Depression on his pension of fifteen dollars a month, supplemented by growing tomatoes, corn, lettuce, cabbage, collards, and other crops for themselves and neighbors. They didn't own the land, but at one time they were farming eighty acres in Middlesex County. Joe attended school when he wasn't working on the farm, but he was kicked out of the seventh grade in 1937 for "settling accounts" with a white boy who called him a derogatory name. In 1937 he spent a year in a Civilian Conservation Corps camp, and then found a job driving a truck—which he was doing when he was drafted in 1943.

That it was the Navy he entered was purely a matter of caprice: "I was drafted," Joe recalled, "and the Navy was a by-chance situation, because there were two of us, close friends. When we went through our physical examination the doctor asked us which one wanted to go into the Army, and neither one of us answered. He just grabbed a stamp and went *bam*! He looked at it and then said, 'All right, move out, soldier.' My buddy happened to be ahead of me and so he got the Army, and I got the Navy."

"I didn't have any choice," another draftee, Cyril Sheppard, a Fourth Division man, remembered. "I wanted to go in the Army. I think it was about thirteen of us that went down to the induction center at the same time and all of us was running right behind one another—we were all trying to stay close so we could be together. No two went to the same place. When they got to me they just sent me over to the Navy office there and the next thing I know I'm in the Navy. I didn't want to be in it."

Another draftee, Jack Crittenden, a seaman in the Second Division, selected the Navy as the lesser evil. "They told me I had a choice between the Marine Corps and the Navy. The man said, 'Hey, we'll take a skinny guy like you, fatten you up, and make a fine marine out of you. And remember, the marines are the first to land, they'll make history right away.' I said, 'First to land?' He said, 'Yeah.' So I said, 'Where's the Navy?' And that's how I came by the Navy."

Some of the draftees did indeed want to be in the Navy—the Navy was their first choice. But as one man explained, there was really little chance for draftees to determine which branch of the service they were sent into: "The branch that needed you the most at the time, that's where you were sent."

Some volunteers also found themselves in the Navy quite by accident. "I was going to volunteer for the Army," Robert Routh, Jr., a Port Chicago survivor recounted. "I wanted to get into the Army cavalry. But on the day I went down to volunteer, the Army recruiting office was closed. I guess they closed at five P.M. and my father and I got there shortly after five. I peered around the corner and the Navy office was standing wide open. I shouted to the guy down there, 'Will the Army open up any more today?' He waved to me and said, 'Come on down here.' And I did."

Martin Bordenave volunteered for the Navy in 1942 when he was only sixteen years old. He wanted to follow in the footsteps of his four older brothers, who had all enlisted in the Navy. He managed to get in, and the fact that he was underage was not discovered for seven months—whereupon he was promptly discharged. He doggedly reenlisted in 1944 when he was old enough.

Most of these young draftees and enlistees were from the rural areas and towns of the South, or from the northern cities. Most were in their teens or early twenties. Some were high school graduates and a very few had attended college. All were trained at the U.S. Naval Training Center at Great Lakes, Illinois.

GREAT LAKES TRAINING CENTER

Located on a sprawling facility near Lake Michigan and forty miles north of Chicago, Great Lakes was the nation's largest naval training center, and the only naval training facility for black sailors during World War II.

According to an official Navy history of Great Lakes, the facility was formally commissioned in July 1911. It had a training capacity of 1,500 men. In World War I the center grew until it became a community of 50,000 people, and in World War II it included a population of 100,000.

After Pearl Harbor, new construction was undertaken at Great Lakes to enlarge the station. The expansion program added eight new training camps, including one—named Robert Smalls*—set aside as a segregated facility for training of black recruits. Each of the new training camps housed 4,500 men.

Lieutenant Commander D. W. Armstrong, son of the founder of Hampton Institute, was sent to head up the program to train black recruits at Great Lakes. The program had been established following the Navy Department's decision in early 1942 to accept black men for general ratings outside of the Steward's Branch.

"There was no disagreement on the policy of segregation," reports the official history of Great Lakes. "That was BuPers [Bureau of Personnel] policy, and no voice was raised at Great Lakes against segregation until late in the war. In 1942 and 1943 there seems to have been no doubt about the wisdom of the segregation policy."

*Robert Smalls was a black Civil War hero. A pilot of a Confederate transport vessel, he ran the ship out of Charleston Harbor in 1862 and delivered it to a Union squadron. Smalls was subsequently made a pilot in the northern Navy.

Although there was no opposition—from the officers—to the policy of segregation, Armstrong was accused by hard-liners of being "not tough enough" and lax about disciplinary problems. Other officers thought that Armstrong favored "special treatment" for blacks, for example, by "having the Negro recruits learn and recite a creed dealing with the advancement of the Negro race, and having them sing spirituals en masse on Sunday nights."

Other kinds of "special treatment" were soon forthcoming. In 1943 Armstrong established a special slacker squad to mete out severe punishment to "troublesome" black recruits. In accordance with the policy of segregation, black regiments competed only among themselves, never with white regiments. Moreover, Armstrong apparently believed that blacks were not qualified to compete against whites for rosters and in school selection.

Special segregated service schools were set up for black recruits at Camp Smalls. Schools for gunner's mates, radiomen, quartermasters, signalmen, yeomen, storekeepers, and cooks and bakers were established in 1942, followed by others in 1943. White officers and, for the most part, white instructors provided training at the schools.

Black recruits, it seems, were of special concern to naval intelligence. The official history of Great Lakes reports:

> Station intelligence watched the Negro regiments carefully. In August 1942 an inflammatory leaflet issued by the Colored Americans National Organization[?] was found in Camp Smalls. In June 1943 when there were race riots in Detroit the Commanding Officer ordered special vigilance. In the next six months several Negroes were investigated for doubtful loyalty and communism. One was found to be "intensely interested" in problems of the Negro; others were interested in "elevating the status of the Negro race." One Yeoman third class was "extremely dissatisfied with the inability of Negroes to advance in the Navy."

Looking for traitors and communists, naval intelligence found only black men who were angered by racism. But that was enough to get some men transferred as potential troublemakers. Sounding a little disappointed, the report concluded: "It appears that white regiments could not very well have assayed less in the way of subversive ideas."

TRAINING AND EXPECTATIONS

Recruits were trained at Great Lakes for two to three months before being shipped out for regular duty. The regimen at Camp Smalls included training in personal hygiene, cleaning of the barracks, marching and drilling, standing guard duty, and practice on the rifle range. Those who were selected for the service school also received training in specialized ratings. There was also an athletics program, including swimming and rowing, in which the recruits participated. There was no training in ammunition handling.

Most of the young recruits arrived at Great Lakes full of curiosity and enthusiasm. Most of them also expected to be trained to go to sea, to become sailors. But this expectation was not to be met for the vast majority of the early recruits. Moreover, some of the northern recruits were immediately disillusioned by the practice of segregation at Great Lakes. "This was where I first ran into discrimination," recalled Percy Robinson, who grew up in Chicago. "When we went to eat, they had a big white house out there where we went. There was two lines. Obviously you stood in one line because all your friends was in this line. So you look around there and there's another line over there that's all white. They were going to eat upstairs on the main floor. All the blacks were going downstairs. It dawned on me that these people were discriminating against me. You see, I grew up in the black belt of Chicago where I wasn't affected by it as much. This was my first experience of racial prejudice in the Navy."

After completion of their basic training the men were shipped out for regular duty. Most would be shipped to ammunition bases, but none of them knew this. In fact, the men had no idea where they were being shipped. The wartime situation made secrecy absolutely necessary. "A slip of the lip will sink a ship," they were told.

BLACK MEN IN THE U.S. MILITARY

Black men have found themselves in every American war since the Revolutionary War. However, black men were never welcomed into the military. Their participation was often allowed only after a fierce struggle with a prejudiced military and political bureaucracy, and then the tasks that black soldiers were assigned were sharply restricted. Black men recruited into the military usually found themselves discriminated against and employed chiefly as laborers and menials serving the needs of white troops and officers.

For example, during the Civil War it was only after a series of military reversals and a strident campaign by black and white abolitionists that the North agreed to use black troops. Some 500,000 blacks contributed their services to the Union cause. Over 300,000 of these were employed as servants and laborers; only 186,000 were actually soldiers. Or again: of some 400,000 blacks who served in World War I, only 10 percent were assigned to combat units; the remaining 360,000 or so were assigned to labor battalions, stevedore battalions, supply regiments, and other service units. During World War II over a million blacks served in the U.S. Armed Forces, including 150,000 black seamen in the Navy. However, virtually all of the black seamen were relegated to mess duty or labor battalions.

Black soldiers were essentially the laborers and menial workers of the American military machine. Indeed, black men have found that their position in the military parallels their position in civilian life: they have been a source of cheap, subordinated labor in both domains. If the military is considered as an employer, then the black struggle within the military has been in large part a fight for the democratization of labor usage. Segregated units, discrimination in pay, discrimination in promotions and ratings, the lack of black officers—these and other grievances of black soldiers corresponded closely to the grievances of black workers in civilian life. But whereas civilian workers may resort to various forms of protest, including strikes, to improve their conditions, the forms of protest allowed in the military are virtually nonexistent—protest being instead treated as insubordination, refusal to obey orders, or even mutiny, and punished accordingly.

While many examples of black servicemen being victimized by

racist forces—such as the Brownsville case of 1906 and the mob attacks on black soldiers during and after World War I—are relatively well known, much less familiar are the instances of active resistance on the part of black servicemen. These acts of resistance are a hidden part of the heritage of popular struggle against racial oppression. If the rebellion by the Port Chicago seamen was perhaps the most spectacular example during World War II, it was not an isolated incident. Within the Navy alone there were several other examples of mass protest and resistance: a two-day hunger strike by one thousand black Seabees (construction battalion workers) in March 1945 to protest Jim Crow practices and lack of promotions; the so-called Guam riot of December 1944 in which black sailors armed themselves to resist harassment by white marines; and the case of fifteen Seabees who in October 1943 were dishonorably discharged because they dared to speak out against discriminatory treatment by the Navy. The Army, too, was racked by frequent racial disorders during the war.

These instances of protest and resistance cannot be separated from the state of the black struggle and the conditions which black servicemen encountered in the military. On the eve of World War II black America was in a watchful, skeptical mood. The Garvey movement had reawakened a sense of racial pride in many Afro-Americans, and the labor and radical movements of the 1930s—in which many blacks participated—had demonstrated the importance of collective action. Italy's invasion of Ethiopia in 1935 and the rise of Hitler's racist regime had attracted black attention to the developing international conflict. Even sports had taken on political overtones with the Joe Louis–Max Schmeling fight and Jesse Owens's Olympic victory in Germany in 1936.

But economic depression and rampant racial discrimination at home continued to preoccupy black leaders, the black press, and the black community in general, and shaped the black response to the war. Unlike World War I, in which a leader such as W. E. B. Du Bois could urge black people to "forget our special grievance and close ranks shoulder to shoulder with our white fellow citizens . . . fighting for democracy," World War II was from the very beginning regarded by most black spokesmen as a struggle on two fronts. Labor leader A. Philip Randolph took the lead in January 1941 when he called for a march on Washington to protest discrimination in the war industries and segregation in the Armed

Forces. Early in 1942 the widely circulated black newspaper the *Pittsburgh Courier* inaugurated its immensely popular "Double V" campaign, calling for victory over the fascists abroad and victory over racism at home. Later that year the *Courier* published the results of an opinion poll among its readers which found that almost 90 percent of those questioned felt that blacks should not soft-pedal demands for complete freedom; indeed, a surprising one third of blacks interviewed in New York believed it was more important to make democracy work at home than to defeat Germany and Japan.

The impatient mood of black America was further apparent in the refusal of blacks in many communities to meekly accept discrimination in housing and employment, or police brutality, or harassment by white mobs. In the summer of 1943 these issues sparked racial disturbances in Los Angeles, Detroit, and New York—the latter precipitated by an incident in which a white policeman shot a black sailor in Harlem. Just a few short miles from Port Chicago in December 1942, the lack of adequate recreational facilities for black servicemen in the town of Vallejo led to a clash between black and white sailors in which several men were injured.

For the most part the U.S. Navy mirrored U.S. society at large. Black men have served in the Navy since the American Revolution, but following World War I the Navy attempted to exclude blacks altogether, replacing them with Filipino stewards. The Navy's growing need for stewards and helpers led to a reversal of this policy in 1932, but black recruits were still limited in numbers and relegated to the most menial tasks. There were no black officers, and the number of black seamen above messman (steward) level was negligible. Black organizations protested this situation, but changes did not occur until the advent of World War II.

Historian Lawrence D. Reddick has argued that during the course of the war the Navy's racial policies evolved through three stages. In the first stage the Navy virtually excluded blacks except in the messman branch. However, as manpower shortages developed and criticism by black leaders mounted, the Navy in April 1942 reluctantly agreed to accept blacks for general service but within a completely segregated system of training and assignments. Finally in 1945, partly as a result of rebellions such as occurred at Guam and Port Chicago, and continued pressure by black organizations and the black press, the Navy announced that it was abolishing segregated training camps and assignments. To be sure, the manpower needs created by the war provided the motive force behind this progression from exclusion to segregation to integration, but Reddick concluded that it was the struggles undertaken by black seamen themselves, supported by the press and civil rights groups, that set the pace and direction of change.

CHAPTER

4

The Base and the Work

The attack on Pearl Harbor on December 7, 1941, thrust the United States suddenly into war with Japan. Within a few moments on that fateful morning, Japanese warplanes sank or seriously damaged six great battleships, three cruisers, and three destroyers, while inflicting greater or lesser damage on many other vessels. In addition, almost two hundred U.S. aircraft at Oahu, Hickam, and Wheeler airfields were destroyed. It was a devastating blow—wrecking half the U.S. Navy—and it dramatically underscored the urgency of expanding West Coast naval facilities.

Even earlier, as the possibility of war with Japan loomed on the horizon and units of the U.S. Fleet were transferred to the Pacific, the need for additional ammunition shipping facilities on the West Coast had become apparent. In 1939 there were only two ammunition depots in the Twelfth Naval District (which included the San Francisco Bay Area in its jurisdiction). The naval ammunition depot at Hawthorne, Nevada, located 120 miles southeast of Reno, manufactured and stored ammunition. The only waterfront depot in the Twelfth District was located at Mare Island, adjacent to the town of Vallejo, twenty miles north of San Francisco. This depot, then the major ammunition preparation and shipping facility op-

37

erated by the Navy's Bureau of Ordnance on the West Coast, was situated in a confined, populated area and could not readily be expanded. Additional ammunition magazines had already been erected along the shore and out into the San Pablo Bay, a branch of San Francisco Bay. Not much more could be added. Clearly, another site for an additional depot was required.

In July 1941 Captain Milton S. Davis, the port director, sent a memorandum to the commandant of the Twelfth Naval District, J. W. Greenslade, outlining the problem and proposing the establishment of another ammunition transshipping terminal "somewhere on San Francisco Bay." Davis suggested that as a temporary expedient, Parr Terminal, No. 4, located at Point San Pablo, could be used to ease the pressure at Mare Island. He then suggested that a new, permanent loading terminal might be constructed at one of two possible sites—Benicia, on the north side of Suisun Bay, or Port Chicago, on the south side. Of the Port Chicago site Davis wrote:

> This site was used during the last War as a shipyard, and several Shipping Board steamers were constructed there. The channel was dredged around the small island just off the site, but no doubt it has silted up during the intervening years and some dredging will probably be required. It has rail connections with the Southern Pacific, Santa Fe, and Western Pacific Railroads. The trackage has deteriorated due to lack of use and will have to be replaced or repaired extensively. A wharf with a shed and trackage must be constructed. Two ship berths alongside are also considered necessary. There is plenty of land suitable for an assembly plant or storage plant should such development be in order. The great value of this site lies in its complete isolation from habitation and industrial activity.

The old shipyard site was less than two miles from the quiet little community of Port Chicago (population about 1,500), which nestled at the foot of a range of hills. Upriver eight miles was the town of Pittsburg, itself overshadowed by the Army's enormous Camp Stoneman, embarkation point for troops shipping out to the

South Pacific. Seven miles downriver lay Martinez, county seat of Contra Costa County. Beyond the hills was the town of Concord, and some thirty miles distant were the thickly populated cities of San Francisco and Oakland. The site at Port Chicago was safely remote from major population centers while being easily accessible by railroad and ship.

Davis asked Commandant Greenslade to appoint a board to follow up on his proposal. He recommended that the board consist of himself as port director, the inspector of ordnance in charge at Mare Island (Captain Nelson H. Goss, whose title was later changed to commanding officer at Mare Island, with Port Chicago as a subsidiary command), and the public works officer of the Twelfth District.

The board recommended by Davis was appointed by the commandant on August 8, 1941. Over the next four months the board investigated the possibilities, and on December 9, 1941, two days after Pearl Harbor, it issued its confidential report recommending that a new loading facility be constructed at Port Chicago.

THE NEW BASE

A naval ammunition magazine at Port Chicago was authorized in February 1942; the site was procured and construction began immediately. According to Captain Goss, the pier at Port Chicago was the first major pier ever built exclusively for the handling and overseas shipment of ammunition. From the beginning, Goss himself was intimately involved with the construction and operation of the new base.

A career naval officer, Nelson Goss was born on April 22, 1882, in Rockville, Indiana. In 1901 he was appointed to the U.S. Naval Academy and graduated in 1905. Goss served as an ensign on various vessels over the next few years. He did well, was promoted to lieutenant in 1910, and lieutenant commander in 1916. During World War I he saw duty in the Philippines, commanding first the U.S.S. *Pompey,* and later the *Villalobos.* He also commanded two destroyers during the war, the U.S.S. *O'Brien* and the *Wadsworth,* earning a Navy Cross for distinguished service in patrol and convoy escort duty. Between the wars Goss commanded half a dozen vessels, had shore duty on both coasts, and was promoted to captain in 1927.

Captain Goss was stationed at Mare Island in March 1938 as inspector of ordnance in charge. (Years before, in 1911, he had been assigned as inspector of ordnance for two years at the Watervliet Arsenal in West Troy, New York.) Goss retired from the Navy in June 1940, but was to continue on active duty until September 1946.

The initial facilities constructed at Port Chicago included a 500-foot-long ships' pier, a smaller barge pier, twenty-seven barricaded sidings to accommodate 203 boxcars, nine storage buildings for inert materials, four barracks for enlisted men, a commissary, and a boiler house. Further, there was a combination administration building, bachelor officers' quarters, dispensary and ship service store. Facilities for marine guards were also included along with various auxiliary structures.

These facilities were completed in November 1942, and boxcars of ammunition began arriving in the first week of December. The first ship to be loaded, the S.S. *Brewer*, moored on December 8, 1942—a year and a day after the attack on Pearl Harbor—and Port Chicago was in business. The *Brewer* took on 3,800 tons of anti-aircraft ammunition destined for allied forces in New Caledonia.

Captain Goss, however, was not satisfied with the approved width of the loading platforms on the new ships' pier. At ten feet wide he thought these too narrow. In May, Goss had written to the Bureau of Ordnance requesting that the pier be widened to accommodate wider platforms. The bureau responded that the time required to widen the pier was prohibitive.

After operations began it was soon discovered in practice that the platforms were indeed too narrow. The pier was originally intended to handle two ships simultaneously, one on each side, but in March 1943 the loading platform on the inboard berth was moved and joined to the outboard loading platform, providing a twenty-foot platform. However, this sacrificed the use of one of the three railway tracks on the pier, and reduced shiploading capacity to one vessel at a time. In this manner the shiploading operation continued until finally, with the growing need for shipping more tonnage, the bureau agreed to widen the pier. This was accomplished in June 1944, and work also began on a marginal pier to further increase the base's capacity. As a result of the widening, two ships could now be loaded simultaneously, one on each side of the pier. This meant that considerably more men, equipment, and ammunition were on the pier at any given time.

PROBLEMS AND PRESSURES

From the outset the new naval magazine was beset with difficulties. One of these was the lack of trained and experienced officers. In testimony before the Naval Court of Inquiry which investigated the explosion, it was revealed that many of the officers at Port Chicago had had no previous training or experience in shiploading, handling ammunition, or commanding enlisted men. Many of the officers were reservists called to active duty from civilian life and given only scanty training of any type. They, like the men under their command, had to "learn by doing" and this no doubt contributed to the likelihood of accidents.

Typical of the junior officers was Lieutenant James Tobin, division officer of the Second Division. An auditor in civilian life, he had no experience of any kind with explosives before arriving at Port Chicago in January 1943. "It was my duty to go down to the dock with the division for the purpose of loading ships with ammunition," he said later. "What I learned about ammunition came through the . . . ensuing months."

Lieutenant Commander Alexander Holman, the officer in charge of training at Port Chicago, would later admit that there was no regular training for officers in ammunition handling. "Some time ago I had discussed with Captain Kinne [the senior officer at Port Chicago] about starting a class for the training of officers. Lieutenant Woodland was agreed upon as being a good officer for this purpose. I had told him to look around and see what samples, charts, diagrams, books, and other things he might get to instruct officers in ammunition, explosives, and things like that, but so far, that had never, up to the time of the explosion, reached a head."

The black enlisted men, who were the bulk of the labor force at Port Chicago, were also untrained for the work they were expected to perform. Their training at Great Lakes had not included any instruction in ammunition loading. As new men arrived at the base, the common practice was to assign a few experienced men to work with them until they had learned their jobs.

There was no facility for giving winch operators special training until late in 1943. Joe Small recounted that he rather casually "picked up" the job of being a winch operator after watching other men operate the machines. He was never trained for the job.

Another man, who was originally stationed at Mare Island, said that he was shipped to Port Chicago as a winch driver even though he had never operated a winch before. He simply held up his hand when an officer was taking names of men who could do storekeeping, carpentry, and winch operation. Fortunately, he was able to learn to operate a winch before he was put to the test in an actual loading situation.

In this regard it is worth noting that weeks before the explosion the longshoremen's union reportedly warned the Navy that there would be a disaster if the Navy continued to use untrained seamen to load ammunition. The waterfront union would not allow a winch driver to handle ammunition unless he had had years of experience with other cargo. The union offered to send experienced longshoremen to train the Navy recruits in safe handling of ammunition, but this offer was apparently ignored by the Navy.

By 1942 the Navy was modifying its racial policies under fire from civil rights groups and others. Blacks were still to be segregated, but they were to be employed more widely in naval installations, particularly as laborers and industrial workers in shore facilities. Consequently, black enlisted personnel were assigned to Port Chicago to load ammunition. Captain Nelson Goss, the commanding officer of Mare Island, of which Port Chicago was a subcommand, was not enthusiastic about receiving black personnel. In communications with higher authorities, Goss had spelled out his personnel requirements. In the first place he opposed the use of contract stevedores, on the grounds that they were too expensive, were subject to union rules regarding working conditions, were under the influence of union leaders, and might harbor saboteurs. Of the other civilian laborers available, Goss noted, many were Filipino and colored—and "most of the men obtainable from these races do not compare favorably with those of the white race." Many of the available white civilians, he believed, were of "enemy alien descent" (Italians?) and therefore security risks. Consequently, Goss recommended that white enlisted personnel be employed at Port Chicago on grounds that they would be less expensive and more manageable than civilian stevedores. But the Bureau of Personnel had other plans.

Goss regarded the black enlisted men as a major problem. He complained that the black recruits "arrived with a chip on their shoulder, if not, indeed, one on each shoulder." He suspected that the black recruits were under subversive influence, because they "insisted they had volunteered for combat duty and they did definitely resent being assigned to what they called 'laborer's work.'" Goss accused the black men of displaying a tendency to question or refuse to obey orders, which resulted in a high percentage of disciplinary actions against them. He also complained that the black personnel were poor workers, capable, in his opinion, of only sixty percent of the efficiency of white workers.

For their part many of the black enlisted men had an equally low opinion of the situation at Port Chicago. To begin with, many of the men were disturbed by the racial discrimination evident in the organization of the base. They resented that only black men were assigned to what were essentially labor battalions charged with doing dangerous and backbreaking work. The men were also distressed by the fact that they could not get the ratings and promotions they thought they deserved. Aside from black petty officers, all the officers at Port Chicago were white. There was little room for upward mobility on a segregated base where it was not possible for a black man to become an officer, and there could be little lateral movement into specialized ratings because basically there was only one job to do—load ammunition.

Pay was another grievance. The men knew that stevedores in civilian life earned considerably more than they were being paid.

Finally, men complained about the lack of recreational facilities. There was little on the base itself (a recreation building was not completed until June 1944, a month before the explosion), the town of Port Chicago was not friendly to blacks, and there was no military transportation from the base to Oakland or San Francisco, only a commercial bus.

Most men accommodated themselves as best they could to the situation. Some sought transfers to other stations. Others complained to petty officers or division officers. Still others vented their anger in acts of individual defiance, but such acts only further confirmed the officers in their habit of ignoring the men's grievances, treating them as simply disciplinary problems.

At least one group of Port Chicago men appealed for outside help: they drafted a letter in 1943 setting forth their grievances and pointing out that morale among the enlisted men had dropped to "an alarming depth." The men asked for a change in Navy policy so that they would have a fair chance to prove their capabilities. The letter ended prophetically: "We, the Negro sailors of the Naval Enlisted Barracks of Port Chicago, California, are waiting for a new deal. Will we wait in vain?" A copy of the letter was sent to Berkeley attorney Walter Gordon, who forwarded it to NAACP headquarters in New York; the reply, if any, was not recorded.

The pressures of the war affected the pace of loading ammunition. Captain Goss determined that a goal of ten tons per hatch per hour should be the objective of the loading crews. In practice this goal was seldom attained, and at the court of inquiry appointed after the explosion there would be considerable discussion of whether such an objective was unreasonably high and might have encouraged unsafe practices and rough handling in an effort to attain it.

For example, when Captain Merrill T. Kinne came on board as officer in charge of Port Chicago in April 1944, he initiated the practice of posting daily average rates of loading for each division in the dock office. Kinne explained that he got the idea for the blackboard from the Navy practice of competition in target practice where scores are kept on the number of shots fired and hits made. "I have never felt," he stated, "that it would be possible to maintain a satisfactory loading rate with the type of enlisted personnel assigned to Port Chicago unless every officer in a supervisory capacity keeps continually in mind the necessity for getting this ammunition out."

In his naval career, Captain Kinne had had only two years' experience with ordnance, and that was more than twenty years earlier, after his 1915 graduation from the Naval Academy. He served seven years in the Navy then, and thereafter until World War II he worked in civilian life as a consulting engineer with no contact whatsoever with explosives. Recalled to active duty in August 1941, Kinne served as an officer on a general cargo ship, the *Republic*. Before coming to Port Chicago he had had no training and little experience with ammunition loading.

It was also disclosed during the court of inquiry that junior officers, according to one of them, "had received some rather sharp letters [from superiors] concerning our lack of efficiency from the standpoint of lack of tonnage." Such criticism, combined with Kinne's blackboard, encouraged the junior officers to promote competition in loading ammunition among the various work divisions. When asked if the posting of tonnage figures encouraged competition and undue haste, the officer above replied: "I would say there is a tendency to be a little rough in order to be a little quicker in stowing." The officer added that at one time the divisions with highest efficiency in loading were rewarded with free movies. Several other junior officers agreed that competition between divisions existed, and some admitted that the practice led to rough and unsafe handling of ammunition.

In general, the issue of safety of procedures was quite problematic at Port Chicago. To begin with, during the entire course of the war the Navy had no loading manual for the guidance of personnel engaged in handling high explosives. Instead, officers at Port Chicago relied on the so-called Red Book which codified a set of safety regulations originally prepared by the Interstate Commerce Commission and designed primarily for peacetime movement of small quantities of explosives. Many of its provisions were inapplicable to wartime conditions confronted by the Navy.

Moreover, there was no organized system for ensuring that officers at Port Chicago were familiar with existing safety regulations beyond occasional informal lectures by the commanding officers. Safety regulations were posted on the pier but not in the enlisted men's barracks, because Captain Kinne did not believe the black seamen were capable of comprehending the regulations. Apparently only two formal lectures on safety were given to the enlisted men in the entire history of Port Chicago before the explosion.

The problem of safety was made worse by conflict between the Mare Island–Port Chicago command and the Coast Guard over who would enforce safety regulations. Existing policy required that a Coast Guard detail be present at the pier to ensure that safe handling procedures were followed. But the Navy commanders felt that a Coast Guard detail was unnecessary and would create confusion and disrupt loading. In October 1943, as an "experiment," a Coast Guard detail was allowed on the pier at Port Chicago. The experiment failed. In the first place, the Coast Guard detail objected to the common practice at Port Chicago of moving bombs by rolling and dropping them (a short distance) into place in the ship's hold. Alternative methods suggested by the Coast Guard representatives were considered "ridiculous" by the cargo placement officers at Port Chicago.

For his part, Captain Goss felt that the presence of the Coast Guard detail led to a divided command on the pier and confused the enlisted men. The situation was not helped by the fact that the white coastguardsmen in effect stood guard over the black Navy enlisted men while not themselves doing any work. After a very short while the Coast Guard detail was withdrawn and ammunition loading at Port Chicago was allowed to proceed in its accustomed manner.

THE WORK ROUTINE

By July 1944 there were 1,431 black enlisted personnel at Port Chicago, 71 officers, and 106 marines who guarded the base. In addition, some 231 civilians were employed as skilled workers such as carpenters, locomotive engineers, and crane operators. Most of the black seamen were organized into eight shiploading divisions consisting of 100 to 125 men each. Each division was headed by white lieutenants with black petty officers acting as foremen of the working gangs. There was also a utility division and a division known as the ship's company consisting of cooks and maintenance men. The ten divisions were housed in two-story wood-frame barracks buildings located about a mile from the loading pier.

Loading went on around the clock in three shifts. Typically, a division would load ships for three consecutive days, seven hours per day. This would be followed by a "duty day" when the division would be assigned other work such as cleaning up the grounds or unloading dunnage (timber used in stowing bombs in boxcars and ships' holds). In the afternoon of the duty day there might be a lecture, an educational film, or a drill, followed by some free time for the men to handle personal chores such as laundry and letter writing. The men were required to stay at the base during duty day in case of emergency. The following day the division would resume loading for three more consecutive days, at the conclusion of which they would have a day's liberty, during which they might leave the base. Consequently, during an eight-day period a division would have six days of ammunition loading, a duty day, and one day of liberty.

On the loading pier the usual practice was to assign one work division to each ship being loaded. The division would be broken into five work gangs, one for each of the ship's hatches. The gangs in turn were divided into two squads, one on the pier and one in the hold of the ship. One man was assigned to operate the winch for that hold and one man would act as hatch attendant to signal the winch operator. Men not actually employed in loading might be assigned as compartment cleaners or mess cooks.

Ammunition was brought onto the pier in railroad boxcars. One or two men were assigned to "break out" the car, using a sledge-hammer and pinch bar to remove dunnage that shored up the bombs.* The rest of the squad would then manhandle the bombs onto the pier—large bombs would be rolled down an incline or removed by electric "mules," and small bombs and boxes of ammunition might be passed hand to hand or transported by hand trucks. The ammunition was placed in nets or on pallets on the pier so it could be hoisted by the ship's booms through the hatch and lowered into the hold, where another squad stowed it away. The bombs were stowed layer by layer, rising slowly from the bottom of the hold to the hatch. During these operations the pier would be jammed with boxcars, locomotives, tons of bombs and high explosives, and men scrambling about everywhere.

The types of ammunition handled included everything from small-arms ammunition to artillery projectiles, depth charges, incendiary bombs, fragmentation bombs, and huge blockbusters weighing as much as two thousand pounds each.

Unloading boxcars and stowing bombs and explosives into ships' holds was backbreaking, heavy labor. Port Chicago was a "work-horse base," as one man put it. "This was solid work," he said. "You'd go down in that ship and you build yourself all the way up—just packing until you find yourself way up on top." "We were a mule team," another man said. Others described the work as hard common labor, rough work. Another man described Port

---

*The men who broke open the boxcars had an extra reward for their efforts: they got the names and addresses of women workers at ammunition plants who sometimes wrote them on the dunnage. More than once a lively correspondence followed.

Chicago as a "slave outfit," adding that "we were considered a cheap labor force from the beginning."

PACE OF WORK

Work did not proceed at a leisurely pace at Port Chicago. "We were pushed," Joe Small said. "The officers used to pit one division against the other, and the officers themselves used to bet on their division putting on more tonnage than the other division. I often heard them argue over what division was beating the others. So we were pushed by the petty officers to get the tonnage in. They were in turn pushed by the officers."

Although no one else mentioned betting among the officers, most agreed that the pace of work was fast and competition between the work divisions was fostered by the officers. "There was always a tonnage thing," one man said. "You always knew what the division in front of you did. If they put on x number of tons that meant you had to do more." Another man described the officers as "tonnage-minded," and he recalled that the officers pushed the men to work faster.

The men were goaded into competition by threats of punishment or losing privileges. Two survivors recalled that the division with the best loading record each week would be given a pennant to fly over their barracks. Another man said the outstanding division might be rewarded with special recreational privileges.

About the only forms of recreation available to the men on the base were ball games, card playing, reading, and writing letters. Some men had access to radios and newspapers such as the *Pittsburgh Courier* and the *Afro-American*.

The chief relief from the drudgery of the work was liberty—free time when the men could leave the base. The town of Port Chicago was segregated and hostile, so the black seamen usually took a bus to Pittsburg, Oakland, or San Francisco in search of nightclubs, bars, and female companionship. Popular locales included Black Diamond Street in Pittsburg, Seventh Street in Oakland, and the Fillmore District of San Francisco. The hottest clubs were Club Seven, Slim Jenkin's, Club Alabama, Club Havana, Sweet's, and Club Jet.

No matter what pleasures liberty might afford, there was always the return to the work at Port Chicago. In search of relief from the daily grind some men got into the spirit of competition. "It got down to where it was a personal thing between the groups," one man recalled. "We used to brag about how many boxcars we unloaded to the next group." When the work shifts changed, men from outgoing divisions sometimes teased and bantered with those coming to the pier, and for a moment besting the other guys almost made up for the drudgery. In any case it was good to joke and laugh and challenge someone else to go one better.

COPING WITH RISK

The enlisted men were certainly not unaware of the dangers inherent in the work of handling ammunition and high explosives. They recounted several incidents that reveal their recognition of the risk involved and the ways they evolved for coping with risk. In particular the men developed various tactics for managing their awareness of the risk of an accidental explosion.

Individual Defiance

Occasionally a man might go AWOL or simply refuse to work. One survivor told the story of an enlisted man who supposedly never worked. "Anytime you see him they're taking him to the brig. They cut your hair, so he was bald-headed. He never saw the inside of one of those ships. He wasn't going to do it. Time he come out of jail, they give him a couple of days to get straight, and when they come for him he just packed up his bag to go to jail. 'I ain't gonna get on those goddamn ships,' he said."

Men who were regarded as causing disciplinary problems were punished by being locked in the brig and sometimes being restricted to bread and water. Most of the enlisted men were well aware of the punishments that could be meted out, because the men made a practice of reading the Blue Jackets' Manual, the official Navy handbook for enlisted men. Indeed, the men were expected by the officers to be able to recite sections from the Blue

Jackets' Manual, and failure to do so successfully could lead to punishment.

Confronting

Some enlisted men, seeing the danger in the work process, confronted the officers with the question of risk. For example, Joe Small said that he confronted superior officers "numerous times" about the danger of an explosion: "I had told everybody in authority that I could get to that we were working dangerously, and one day that place would blow up. The lieutenant gave me a manual that contained a diagram of a five-hundred-pound bomb that was supposed to be totally harmless without the detonator in it. We had a discussion about it. I said, 'Won't concussion blow this thing up?' He said it's impossible—'it cannot blow up without this charge in the head of it.' I didn't believe it. Every time we got in an argument over it, it wound up with him telling me that if it does blow up I wouldn't know anything about it."

Enlisted men sometimes confronted each other over the danger of an explosion. One man, who arrived at the base less than two months before the explosion, described an incident he experienced in unloading a boxcar: "I tell you this. Them guys didn't have the training; they didn't know what they were doing. I'm standing right up there and they got them big bombs, bombs you can't even get your arms around. You hook the winch on there and bring it out. Then the winch operator yanked it suddenly so it hit the sides of that steel railroad car, bam! bam! bam! I said, 'Goddamn, man, can't you do better than that?' He says, 'Oh, man don't worry about that. I felt the same way when I first came here. But these things ain't got no fuses in them.' I said, 'I don't care about the fuse, they got TNT in them!' "

In this instance the winch operator, a veteran at the base, attempted to reassure the novice worker in the same way as the officer in the earlier incident—discounting the risk on the grounds that the bomb was defused.

In both of these situations the confronters did not accept the discounting of risk that was proffered to them. However, for most of the enlisted men, discounting of risks was the major social-psychological mechanism by means of which they coped with their recognition of danger.

Discounting

Discounting is the social process by which the men came to lower their estimation of the risks involved in ammunition loading. Most of the enlisted men, upon first arriving at Port Chicago, were quite fearful of the explosives they were expected to handle. Over time the men learned, through interaction with other men and the officers, to manage their fear through the discounting process. Contrary to the example cited above, some men readily accepted the officers' assurances that the bombs could not explode because they had no detonators. Others were influenced by the attitude of the veteran workers who obviously discounted the risk. Still others witnessed or were told about minor accidents that did not result in an explosion, and consequently they lowered their estimation of the risk. One respondent told of seeing two sixteen-inch projectiles that apparently had been damaged in transit without exploding. After a couple of experiences like that, he said, the men "never really felt it was really that dangerous."

Another man described a frightening incident that he experienced: "We had some funny experiences that we had to learn about things—like sixteen-inch projectiles, that's one the battleship shoots. Well, each battleship has a different color dye in the nose of its projectiles. This is so that if two or three battleships shoot a target and one of them is off, they can tell by the color of the explosion which one is off. This dye is under pressure at the tip of the projectile. Well, if you butt the nose, if you break the seal on it, it squirts out. And if you see a bomb sitting there going *psssssst*, it looks like it's going to explode. Now that happened to us one time. They should have told us about that; we should have gone to school or something to learn about something like this. The first time it happened three or four guys broke their legs trying to get out of that damned hold. We were down in the hold working and they dropped one of these things down there. You spin them around to get them in the hold and sometimes you lose control because they are wet, and this thing hit against the bulkhead and started going *psssst*. Red stuff started coming out. Well, hell you had ten, twelve guys trying to get out of the hold at the same time. You can't do it. Some guys broke their legs trying to get out of that hold. And then the others laughed at us because we weren't familiar with the situation. Evidently it had happened before, see. It was a kind of funny joke to some people."

Gradually, through the process of talking and sharing experiences among the enlisted men, combined with the exhortations and reassurances of the officers, the apparent risks of the work were slowly discounted, enabling most of the men to manage their fears and accommodate themselves to performing extremely dangerous work.

COPING WITH GRIEVANCES

Aside from dangerous working conditions, the enlisted men at Port Chicago, as at other military installations, had a number of grievances that distressed them. Chief among these was racial discrimination—the fact that all the commissioned officers at the base were white and all the men who actually did the heavy work of handling ammunition were black. Many men had expected to be sent to sea, and they were angry over finding themselves instead assigned to a "labor battalion" at an ammunition depot. The men were also disturbed by the restrictions on ratings, promotions, and transfers, the low pay (compared with civilian stevedores), and the lack of recreational facilities. Several processes emerged among the enlisted men for coping with their grievances.

Confrontation

Enlisted men sometimes attempted to take their complaints through the chain of command, confronting petty officers with their grievances. The result of this action, according to several men, was that their complaints were simply allowed to "get lost in the shuffle." No action was taken and the complaint simply "died."

Some men were particularly angered by what they regarded as

the "incompetence" of the petty officers, whom they viewed as "Uncle Toms" and "slave drivers," who were easily "handled" by the white officers. In their view the petty officers had fundamentally different interests from the enlisted men, and the two were sometimes in an antagonistic relationship that did not aid in resolving grievances.

Sometimes the enlisted men themselves took action to dramatize a particular complaint. Several minor work slowdowns and stoppages had occurred in the past. As one man put it, "You couldn't strike, you couldn't quit, so you just slowed down." Slowdowns and stoppages had been prompted by dissatisfaction with food, promotion policy, and racist slurs directed at the enlisted men. These actions were a form of collective confrontation and were precursors of the work stoppage that occurred after the explosion.

Balancing

Often the enlisted men coped with their grievances by the mechanism of balancing. Balancing refers to the social process by which the men decided that certain grievances were offset by the perceived benefits of Navy life. For example, two survivors listed several grievances concerning racial practices during training and at Port Chicago, and then followed this list with the statement that the grievances were "balanced out a little" by the fact that black men were now being admitted to the seaman's branch of the Navy for the first time. One of the men added: "Being in the Navy is being able to sleep between white sheets and have three square meals a day, hot meals; this was a privilege that black men hadn't enjoyed and so we didn't put up much of a squawk about [grievances]." The men griped among themselves but that was generally where it ended. Another survivor balanced his grievances against the opportunity to prove his worth as a black man by serving his country in time of war.

The process of balancing did not remove grievances; rather it was a coping tactic that acted to reduce tension and minimize confrontations between the enlisted men and the officers over grievances. Balancing, like discounting, enabled the enlisted men to tolerate the stresses that they encountered at Port Chicago.

Apathy

Some men—perhaps most of the men at some time—simply fell into apathy, feeling that nothing could be done about their grievances. As one man put it: "We knew the situation shouldn't have been that way but it appeared that it was out of our reach." "There were a lot of complaints," said another, "but we were powerless to do anything about this."

ATTITUDES TOWARD THE WAR

The enlisted men's attitudes toward the war effort ranged from patriotism to indifference. The men's patriotism was often tied to their hopes of improving the situation of blacks in the United States. One survivor, who volunteered for the Navy, said that he wanted to "get in there and help to prosecute the war." He added that he hoped to have a "hand in making this a better place for blacks to live in this country." He felt that many enlisted men were disappointed at being denied the "privilege" of combat duty. "We came to fight, let us fight," was their attitude, he said.

A variation of this theme was reflected by Jack Crittenden, a draftee, who recalled a patriotic oration he delivered at his high school graduation: "Remember Pearl Harbor. It was Dorie Miller* who was not trained to fight but picked up a gun and fought for his country. He proved himself capable. And when more black men are given the opportunity to serve their country they will prove themselves worthy of the trust placed in them. Give them a chance! Let previous condition of servitude be no hold back. A man is still a man! All our men are facing the same enemy under the same flag. America owes it to them to see that they come back to the same opportunity."

Another man, who was initially assigned as a mess attendant aboard a yard minesweeper, voiced dissatisfaction with the Navy's earlier common practice of assigning black men to the Steward's Branch. "When I come to fight," he said, "I don't want to come

---

*Dorie Miller, a black Navy mess attendant, was one of the first heroes of the war. During the attack on Pearl Harbor, Miller manned a machine gun on the *West Virginia* and shot down four enemy planes. He was later awarded the Navy Cross for bravery.

fighting with pots and pans." Subsequently he requested a transfer to Great Lakes, where he went to gunnery school, and then, to his dismay, he ended up at Port Chicago loading ammunition.

For many of the men the war was remote, both physically and psychologically. "It wasn't discussed," one man said. "We weren't concerned about it. I mean, I wasn't. I knew that my job supported the war, but this was what I was expected to do in my job. It was my job and I did it. If the Japanese and the Americans got in trouble over in Iwo Jima or Okinawa or somewhere, we knew about it but we weren't concerned. I had no brothers over there; I had no close friends over there. We were more concerned about our own little clique, working, and not being punished for not doing enough work. We were just loading ammunition. My concern with the war started when a bomb came out of a boxcar and ended when I set it down in the hold of a ship."

In sum, the attitudes of the enlisted men—including those later charged with mutiny—ran the gamut from patriotism to indifference. This is not surprising, since such a range of views was to be found in the general black community at that time, and the Port Chicago men, through letters, radios, and newspapers, were at least vaguely aware of the sentiments of the larger black community.

CHAPTER

5

The Explosion and After

The fateful, moonless night of Monday, July 17, 1944, was clear and cool. A slight breeze was blowing from the southwest. Two cargo ships were tied up at the Port Chicago pier, and under floodlights work was proceeding at full speed.

Tied to the inboard, landward side of the pier facing downstream was the *E. A. Bryan*. Taking on explosives night and day, the *Bryan* had been moored at Port Chicago for four days. Ninety-eight men of Division Three were hard at work loading the ship, and by ten o'clock that night the ship was loaded with some 4,600 tons of ammunition and high explosives.

On the outboard side of the pier, turned into the current, was the *Quinalt Victory*. Brand-new, it was preparing for its maiden voyage. The *Quinalt Victory* had moored at Port Chicago at about six that evening. More than one hundred men of the Sixth Division, many of them also new arrivals at Port Chicago, were busy rigging the ship in preparation for loading. Loading of ammunition was due to begin at midnight.

In addition to the enlisted men there were present on the ships and pier nine Navy officers, sixty-seven members of the crews of the two ships along with an armed guard detail of twenty-nine men, the crew members of a Coast Guard fire barge also tied up at the pier, a marine sentry, and a train crew of three civilians. The pier was congested with men, equipment, a locomotive and sixteen railroad boxcars, and about 430 tons of bombs and projectiles waiting to be loaded.

At about 9:30 P.M. Captain Kinne left the administrative offices and drove out to the pier to have a look at the new ship. At the pier he met Lieutenant Commander Holman, the loading officer, who informed him that the new ship was good and clean, having just arrived from the builders, and that the loading of the *Bryan* was coming along satisfactorily. Kinne picked up Holman and the two drove to the officers' quarters.

Meanwhile, Lieutenant Commander Glen Ringquist, Holman's assistant, continued to observe the work. Ringquist noticed that the propeller on the *Quinalt Victory* was slowly turning over, and he asked another officer to be sure it had stopped before they started loading. Ringquist then walked over beside the *Bryan* and watched the loading operation. In the No. 5 hold forty-millimeter shells were being loaded. Fragmentation cluster bombs were being hoisted into the No. 4 hold. Huge 1,000-pound bombs were being lowered into the No. 3 hold, and depth bombs, used against submarines, were being hoisted into the No. 2. Ringquist saw that incendiary bombs, weighing 650 pounds each, were being loaded into the No. 1 hold. These latter bombs had their activating mechanisms, or fuses, installed. Considered especially dangerous—"hot cargo"—they were being loaded gingerly, one bomb at a time. Ringquist noticed that the men were having some difficulty getting the bombs out of the boxcar because they were wedged in so tightly.

After observing the work for a few minutes Ringquist started to return to the dock office. A base station wagon, making routine rounds, picked him up, and he asked the driver to take him to Building A-1, the administration building, which was off the pier some distance away. The time was about 10:15 P.M; Ringquist and his driver were probably the last individuals to leave the pier before the explosion.

THE EXPLOSION

In the enlisted men's barracks it was quiet; many men were in their bunks. Shortly after 10:18 P.M. disaster struck.

Cyril Sheppard, an enlisted man in the Fourth Division barracks, described what happened in the next moments: "I was sitting on the toilet—I was reading a letter from home. Suddenly there were two explosions. The first one knocked me clean off. . . . I found myself flying toward the wall. I just threw my hands up like this, then I hit the wall. Then the next one came right behind that, Phoom! Knocked me back on the other side. Men were screaming, the lights went out and glass was flying all over the place. I got out to the door. Everybody was . . . that thing had . . . the whole building was turned around, caving in. We were a mile and a half away from the ships. And so the first thing that came to my mind, I said, 'Jesus Christ, the Japs have hit!' I could have sworn they were out there pounding us with warships or bombing us or something. But one of the officers was shouting, 'It's the ships! It's the ships!' So we jumped in one of the trucks and we said let's go down there, see if we can help. We got halfway down there on the truck and stopped. Guys were shouting at the driver from the back of the truck, 'Go on down. What the hell are you staying up here for?' The driver says, 'Can't go no farther.' See, there wasn't no more docks. Wasn't no railroad. Wasn't no ships. And the water just came right up to . . . all the way back. The driver couldn't go no farther. Just as calm and peaceful. I didn't even see any smoke."

Lying in his bunk, Joe Small was not yet asleep when he heard both explosions: "I didn't know what the first one was—and the second one just disintegrated the barracks. It picked me up off the bunk—I was holding on to my mattress—and flipped me over. I hit the floor with the mattress on top of me. That's why I escaped injury. The glass and debris that fell hit the mattress rather than me. I got one minor cut.

"Other fellows were cut and bleeding all over the place. I helped some of the men that were injured. One fellow's feet were bleeding and I gave him my shoes. Another fellow had a cut all the way down his arm, and I put a tourniquet on it to try to stop the bleeding. There were no medics around; it was chaos."

Jack Crittenden, who was scheduled to do guard duty that night, had just walked into the administration building: "I'm over there with the petty officer, sitting there in the window, telling him my name and all that. Then this damned thing happened. Talk about light traveling faster than sound. . . . Well, the first thing was this great big flash, and then something must have hit me. I found myself outside of that building and I don't remember going out of no window or climbing out of it. But I was outside and with only one little scar on my arm. You're talking about torn up. Everybody felt at that point that it was another Pearl Harbor—not that the ships had blown up, because you didn't think about that at that point, because of the building that you had been in and the barracks and all that—caved in, windows busted out, blown out and all that kind of thing. People running and hollering. You know a bunch of guys were sleeping in the barracks. The barracks had a lot of windows, lower and upper deck, whole side was windows. And they were blown to pieces. Some guys lost their sight; others were badly cut. Finally they got the emergency lights together. Then some guys came by in a truck and we went down to the dock, but when we got there we didn't see no dock, no ship, no nothing."

Seventeen-year-old Robert Routh, Jr., was blinded by the explosion: "When taps was sounding that evening I put my writing gear away and went to wash up and put on my Noxema—being a teenager I had some of those blemishes on my face. I came back and I was lying on my bunk. It would usually take about twenty minutes to quiet the men down after lights-out. And shortly after, probably ten-twenty, there was this tremendous explosive sound. I was looking to my right, I had my head pillowed on my arm looking away from the explosion. I quickly jumped up to look and see what was going on and there was a second explosion—all these tremendous beautiful flashes in the sky. That's when the flying glass hit my face and entered my eyes. It did it in such a strange way, inasmuch as I never felt any pain from it. It lacerated the left eye so badly that it was removed that night. The right eye had a laceration, just one laceration in the eye itself that traveled across part of the pupil and cornea allowing the vitreous fluid to drain, which left me with split vision in that eye. They were able to put a suture in there. Of course, sutures leave permanent scar tissue, and the scar tissue eventually caused the sight to leave me completely."

Captain Kinne was in his room at the BOQ when the explosion occurred: "I was sitting there reading when the first blast went off. The first blast impressed me more as the slamming of an enormous door. At any rate, it jarred me out of my chair or I jumped up, and started for the door. The lights, of course, had gone off, and before I got to the door I turned around and felt my way into my bedroom to find a flashlight. A second blast went off while I was going into the bedroom. The flashlight was missing. I started out through the door again and fell down through a hole made by a five-inch low order which was next morning found in an upholstered chair in the BOQ. I then made my way down the stairs, which faced toward Port Chicago. I noticed a fire burning out in the vicinity of the railroad tracks in Port Chicago.

"My first reaction, of course, was that there had been an explosion at the docks or in the ship, and when I saw this fire, and realized that the BOQ was still standing, I momentarily got the hope that it was a car of explosives which had gone off on the tracks outside of the magazine. I got in my car and drove to the main gate and asked the sentries on duty there what had happened. They said there had been an explosion at the dock. I asked what the fire was outside and they said it was nothing but a grass fire, so I headed my car for the dock, and as I went back past the BOQ I was hailed by Lieutenant Beck, duty officer for the barracks. He jumped in with me and at the same time one or two other officers got in the back seat. We started for the docks and found that no one had any lights. As we went past A-1, one of the officers stated that he knew where there were some flashlights in A-1, so he got out to get them. I waited one or two minutes for him and he did not return and, seeing that A-1 was pretty well wrecked, I decided to waste no time . . . so Lieutenant Beck and I proceeded to the dock.

"When we got there, by the lights of the lamps of the car, I saw that the joiner shop at the end of the dock was completely demolished. A marine and a civilian, apparently rather badly cut, were coming out of the wreckage and said there were other men inside. I told them to jump in the car and left Lieutenant Beck there with some other officers who had arrived in other transportation, directed them to get portable floodlights on the joiner shop as soon as possible, and start taking the men out of the wreckage, said that I would take the two injured men to the dispensary and get a working party to help them. I drove the two injured men to the dispensary and found that Lieutenant Hodgen, executive officer of the barracks, and the division officer of the barracks were taking care of the wounded with the assistance of Dr. Carson, the senior medical officer.

"I found that the barracks had been evacuated, that the injured were being taken care of and the more seriously injured were being taken to hospitals outside of the magazine, while Dr. Carson was administering first aid on the lawn in front of the dispensary, that the uninjured personnel were being mustered, and that there was no appearance of panic or disorder. I accordingly instructed Mr. Hodgen to have a working party of about fifty men sent to the dock to assist in clearing the debris from the joiner shop and locating any injured men there. I also found that a search was being made of all buildings in the barracks area to determine whether any injured were there. I then obtained a flashlight and returned to the dock, and went out on the pier as far as possible and found that there was no vestige of either the ship or of the shiploading pier except for a little wreckage. I returned and found that flood-lights had been installed, that there was light on the joiner shop and the working party was going after the injured there, and found there was a bigger working party than was needed because the marines had also sent a working party down in the meantime. I consequently ordered approximately half the working party to return to barracks and left the rest there to continue their rescue operations. I returned to the barracks and found that everything there was in as good order as could be expected under the circumstances."

Lieutenant Commander Ringquist was in the base station wagon on the way to Building A-1 when he heard the first sound of trouble: "Just prior to arriving at Building A-1, I heard a terrific crash . . . that sounded . . . it had a very metallic ring and sounded very hollow, followed by a noise that sounded of breaking timbers. [Ringquist would later testify that he thought this noise, which he heard before the first explosion, was caused by the falling of one of the jumbo booms on the ships.] This was immediately followed by a flash which appeared orange in color, and a very sharp report. The driver grabbed his ear and I thought he lost control of the car momentarily. But prior to this, a considerable pressure had been built up in the station wagon. I was sitting in the rear with the windows closed; the driver's window was open. I realized that this explosion had come from the dock. The sky was illuminated with a very yellow glow.

"I immediately asked the driver to stop the car . . . and I told him to get out of the car and follow me. I ran back hoping to be able to see the ship, but I realized that with the illumination increasing that the ship was going to blow shortly.

"I could not observe [the explosion of the *Bryan*] from the start, as the building obstructed my view, but after the column seemed to have reached about sixteen hundred feet I could observe the smoke and it seemed to me at about two thousand feet a red flame rolled out of this cloud. Prior to this I had noticed that a considerable flame shot off to my right from this column . . . this was in the direction of the town of Port Chicago. This flame and smoke appeared to me to rise to about three to four thousand feet and then darkness set in, and fragments started to fall, which appeared to me to be of a duration of approximately thirty seconds.

"Upon hearing no more fragments fall, I got up and ran to where I could see the pier, which was in total darkness. I ran back to the station wagon and we drove slowly up by the boxcars and barricades to look for fires. I observed no fires until I reached the barracks. There was one fire across the railway tracks. Men were coming out of the barracks and there were no lights at that time except we used the station wagon lights and turned the lights on from the various trucks, until such time that we brought out the portable trailer lights, which I assisted in setting in position. Several men seemed to be seriously wounded. The doctors were taking care of these. Some civilian came to me . . . I believe he was working on the station . . . and he asked me what he should do. I told him to get to the nearest telephone, notify Mare Island and the Twelfth Naval District and the Army, if they were in the vicinity; that we needed medical assistance, lights, and water.

"I then went over to the doctor and asked him if he needed any assistance and he stated that he thought he could take care of the situation. I went over to the BOQ and, with the aid of matches, I discovered the linen locker and carried over an armload of clean linen for the medical department. In the meantime, I had noticed Captain Kinne in his car driving toward the piers. This man that I had sent out came back in about ten minutes and stated that there was one line clear in Port Chicago and the operator was notifying these various activities. I should judge that the first outside ambulances arrived in about thirty minutes. In the meantime, the wounded were being placed in trucks and station wagons and removed. A Greyhound bus was brought in and loaded down with the wounded and sent to the Army post, which I found out later."

Seismograph machines at the University of California at Berkeley recorded two jolts with the force of a small earthquake. They occurred about seven seconds apart shortly before 10:19 P.M. A first, smaller explosion (which appeared to some witnesses to occur on the pier itself) was followed by a cataclysmic blast as the *E. A. Bryan* exploded like one gigantic bomb, sending a column of fire and smoke and debris climbing twelve thousand feet into the night sky, with hundreds of exploding shells making it look like a huge fireworks display.

An Army Air Force plane happened to be flying over at the time. The copilot described what he saw: "We were flying the radio range from Oakland headed for Sacramento. We were flying on the right side of the radio range when this explosion occurred. I was flying at the time and looking straight ahead and at the ground when the explosion occurred. It seemed to me that there was a huge ring of fire spread out to all sides, first covering approximately three miles—I would estimate it to be about three miles—and then it seemed to come straight up. We were cruising at nine thousand feet above sea level and there were pieces of metal that were white and orange in color, hot, that went quite a ways above us. They were quite large. I would say they were as big as a house or a garage. They went up above our altitude. The entire explosion seemed to last about a minute. These pieces gradually disintegrated and fell to the ground in small pieces. The thing that struck me about it was that it was so spontaneous, seemed to happen all at once, didn't seem to be any small explosions except in the air. There were pieces that flew off and exploded on all sides. A good many stars and [it] looked like a fireworks display."

Nearby on the river that night were two other vessels. A Coast Guard patrol boat, the *Miahelo*, piloted by Robert Dollar, was plowing upstream about five hundred yards from the pier. Farther away a small tanker, the S.S. *Redline*, was following the current downstream. The enormous blast from Port Chicago smashed into the small Coast Guard boat, wrecking the wheelhouse and almost capsizing the vessel. Three stunned crewmen struggled up from below to find a bleeding Robert Dollar lying on the deck, his body slashed by glass and fragments. Moments later a thirty-foot wall of water washed over the vessel, but again, miraculously, the *Miahelo* survived. The superstructure of the *Redline* was also heavily damaged, and the boat lost power. Later it was discovered that a sixteen-inch shell had smashed into the engine room of the *Redline*, but—another miracle—it failed to explode.

At the Roe Island lighthouse, keeper Erven Scott, his wife, Bernice, and the assistant keeper were just finishing a late cup of coffee. The explosion shook the house violently and broke all the windows. Mrs. Scott grabbed her two children and sent her husband upstairs for the baby. As he ran up the stairs Erven Scott saw a plume of smoke and flame rising above Port Chicago. He also saw a twenty-to-thirty-foot-high wave rolling toward the lighthouse from the direction of the explosion. He watched the wave for a moment, then dashed back downstairs with the baby. By the time the tidal wave reached Roe Island it had expended most of its energy; still it hit with sufficient force to push the lighthouse boat forty feet up on the beach.

Throughout the Bay Area startled citizens were awakened by an ominous low rumbling accompanied by the shaking of the earth; it felt much like an earthquake. Indeed, this was what many thought at first had happened—another of San Francisco's frequent earthquakes had struck. But in towns like Martinez, Pittsburg, and Benicia, close enough to be hit by the powerful shock wave that shattered windows, people knew it was no earthquake.

The *E. A. Bryan* was literally blown to bits—very little of its wreckage was ever found that could be identified. The *Quinalt Victory* was lifted clear out of the water by the blast, turned around, and broken into pieces. The stern of the ship smashed back into the water upside down some five hundred feet from where it had originally been moored. The Coast Guard fire barge was blown two hundred yards upriver and sunk. The locomotive and boxcars disintegrated into hot fragments flying through the air. The 1,200-foot-long wooden pier simply disappeared.

Everyone on the pier and aboard the two ships and the fire barge was killed instantly—320 men, 202 of whom were black enlisted men. (Only 51 bodies sufficiently intact to be identified were ever recovered.) Another 390 military personnel and civilians were injured, including 233 black enlisted men. This single stunning disaster accounted for more than 15 percent of all black naval casualties during the war.

Property damage, military and civilian, was estimated at more than $12 million.

In the Port Chicago movie theater that night 192 patrons were watching the war movie *China*. Joe Meyer, owner-manager of the theater, was operating the projector. A bombing scene flashed on the screen—and suddenly the north wall of the theater buckled in. Frightened people dashed outside as the roof began to sag. They were lucky; only a few suffered minor scratches. As the startled patrons stumbled outside they were amazed to see a huge plume of fire and smoke rising above the Navy pier.

The town of Port Chicago was heavily damaged by the explosion. Most of the small community's three hundred homes were damaged—some wrecked—as were twenty-seven stores and business establishments. The town was bombarded by falling debris from the ships, including undetonated bombs and jagged chunks of smoldering metal, some weighing hundreds of pounds. Fortunately, none of the town's citizens was killed, although 109 people suffered injuries, the most common of which were lacerations due to flying glass and debris. Many townspeople suffered damage to their eyes as they looked through windows at the blast; twelve permanently lost the sight of an eye. Rescue assistance was rushed from nearby towns and military bases. It was a devastating blow to the small community—one from which it never recovered.

The naval base itself was reduced to a shambles, but there was no panic. The survivors picked themselves up, organized rescue efforts and helped the injured, and put out small fires started by flaming debris. One group of black seamen and officers bravely fought and extinguished a fire that had started in a boxcar loaded with explosives. If the boxcar had exploded, it might well have set off a chain of explosions in nearby boxcars and possibly killed more men.

The Port Chicago explosion was the worst home-front disaster of the war. The explosive force of the blast was equivalent to five kilotons of TNT, on the same order of magnitude as the atomic bomb that would be dropped on Hiroshima just over a year later. During World War I there had been a worse home-front disaster involving munitions when an ammunition ship and a freighter collided and exploded in 1917 in the harbor of Halifax, Nova Scotia. More than sixteen hundred people in the city and on the ships died as a thousand buildings were destroyed and seventy-five acres razed by the blast and ensuing fires.

Several disastrous explosions occurred in World War II, including one in Lower New York Bay when the destroyer *Turner* blew up in January 1943, and another later in the same year when twenty-five people were killed in an ammunition explosion at the Norfolk, Virginia, naval air station. The magnitude of the Port Chicago disaster, however, was far greater than these, and would have been even worse had it not been for the relative isolation of the base from population centers. As it was, to those who survived, it was no doubt the most frightening experience of their lives.

During the night and early morning of July 18 the injured were removed to hospitals, and many of the uninjured seamen were evacuated to nearby stations, chiefly to Camp Shoemaker in Oakland. Others remained at Port Chicago to clear away debris and search for what could be found of bodies.

The search for bodies was grim work. Jack Crittenden recalled the experience: "I was there the next morning. We went back to the dock. Man, it was awful; that was a sight. You'd see a shoe with a foot in it, and then you would remember how you'd joked about who was gonna be the first one out of the hold if something went wrong. You'd see a head floating across the water—just the head—or an arm. Bodies . . . just awful. A piece of the ship the size of a table went into the concrete where the officers lived. We couldn't move it.

"That was quite an experience the next day. That thing kept you from sleeping at night. You had buddies of yours that left your division and were transferred to the division that worked on the ship that night. Then again this is just one of those tragedies of war. I'm saying that now, but it wasn't that way then—it was awful."

Some two hundred of the enlisted men volunteered to remain at the base to help with the cleanup operation.

Three days after the explosion Captain Kinne issued a statement praising the black seamen for their behavior during the disaster. Stating that the men had acquitted themselves with "great credit," he added: "Under those emergency conditions regular members of our complement and volunteers from Mare Island displayed creditable coolness and bravery."

Rear Admiral Carleton H. Wright, the new commandant of the Twelfth Naval District, also commended the men:

I am gratified to learn that, as was to be expected, Negro personnel attached to the Naval Magazine Port Chicago performed bravely and efficiently in the emergency at that station last Monday night. These men, in the months that they served at that command, did excellent work in an important segment of the District's overseas combat supply system. As real Navy men, they simply carried on in the crisis attendant on the explosion in accordance with our Service's highest traditions.

Four Port Chicago seamen and one black enlisted man from Mare Island were awarded medals for their heroic conduct in fighting the ammunition boxcar fire that broke out after the explosion. These men were James A. Camper, Jr., William E. Anderson, Richard L. McTerre, Effus S. Allen, and John A. Haskins, Jr. Captain Kinne was also awarded a Bronze Star.

Memorial services for the dead were scheduled to be held on July 30, and in Washington steps were being taken to compensate the families of the victims. A proposal was presented in Congress to grant the families up to $5,000 in compensation. However, when Mississippi Representative John Rankin objected to the plan because most of the beneficiaries would be black, Congress in its wisdom reduced the maximum allowable grant to $3,000.

Meanwhile, as Navy Seabees scrambled to build a new pier at the naval depot, the town of Port Chicago was picking itself up and beginning to think of rebuilding. Gas service was restored after the mains were checked and found undamaged. The Port Chicago Hotel, severely damaged, was nevertheless reopened two days after the disaster and its nine residents permitted to return. Joe Meyer was planning to rebuild his theater. The town's one grocery store—nearly wrecked, much of its stock condemned—still had not reopened, but a citizens' committee on rebuilding was working with the owner to get the store back in operation.

Army demolition teams scoured the countryside collecting unexploded bombs and fragments, while the Red Cross rushed in workers and eighty thousand board feet of lumber for emergency repairs to the town. In late July a claims board was set up by the Navy to assess the total amount of damage.

Almost all of the town's businesses and ninety percent of its homes had sustained damage. Homeowners and business people worried about who would pay for the damage—insurance companies or the government.

At the end of July the Navy announced plans to greatly expand the base at Port Chicago into one of the country's largest supply bases. A $20-million budget was planned for the expansion, the announcement said.

The Navy's expansion plans and the issue of damage claims quickly polarized the town's citizens into feuding factions distinguished chiefly by degree of greed. One group frankly wanted the Navy to buy the town outright—at a healthy price—and rebuild it as living quarters for personnel at the expanded base. A second, more vociferous faction was willing to stay put, but strongly urged that in addition to covering repair costs the Navy should also provide generous compensation for mental and physical suffering. Only a minority of the town's citizens, it seems, was willing to accept payment only for the actual costs of repairs.

With insurance companies balking at covering losses, residents appealed to Congress to pass a bill directing the government to assume responsibility. A bill was presented, initially allowing claims for damage up to $5,000, but this was the bill Congressman Rankin disliked when he discovered it would also benefit the survivors of the dead black sailors. His reduction of the maximum benefit to $3,000 ironically meant that the white Port Chicago citizens could get no more than that amount in their individual claims. The townspeople were outraged.

COURT OF INQUIRY

Four days after the Port Chicago disaster, on July 21, a Naval Court of Inquiry was convened to "inquire into the circumstances attending the explosion." The inquiry was to establish the facts of the situation, and the court was to arrive at an opinion concerning the cause or causes of the terrible explosion. The court was comprised of three senior naval officers, Captains Albert G. Cook, Jr., John S. Crenshaw, and William B. Holden. A judge advocate, Lieutenant Commander Keith Ferguson, was responsible for assembling evidence and witnesses for interrogation.

Both Captain Goss and Captain Kinne were present throughout the proceedings as "interested parties," which meant that they were allowed to present evidence and examine witnesses "in the same way as a defendant."

The inquiry stretched out over a month, and 125 witnesses were called to testify. The court heard testimony from survivors and eyewitnesses, other Port Chicago personnel, ordance experts, inspectors who checked the ships during loading, and others. Despite the fact that only black enlisted men actually handled the bombs and ammunition and operated the winches, only five black witnesses were called to testify.

The proceedings quickly became contentious as the key issue that emerged was the question of output versus safety. A sharp disagreement developed between the Navy brass, Goss and Kinne, and the captain of the port and the port director, who were responsible for the safe movement of vessels through San Francisco Bay. The heart of the dispute centered on whether unsafe loading practices were employed at Port Chicago, and why no Coast Guard loading detail was present the night of the explosion. Goss contended that the representatives of the Coast Guard and the port director's office were inexperienced personnel who were unable to properly supervise the loading operation and themselves created problems for the work.

However, Goss admitted that after the unsuccessful "experiment" with the presence of a Coast Guard detail in October 1943, he met with the port director, who warned him: "Conditions are bad up there [at Port Chicago]; you've got to do something about it. . . . If you aren't careful, something's going to happen, and you'll be held responsible for it." The port director recommended that contract stevedores be brought in to do the loading at Port Chicago. Goss responded that he already knew about the problematic conditions at Port Chicago, that he needed experienced officers, and that contract stevedores were not available. The captain of the port, who was also present at this meeting, decided to withdraw the Coast Guard detail because conditions were so bad that he was unwilling to take responsibility for it. Goss persisted in his view that enlisted personnel should be able to equal the work of professional stevedores. (Apparently, contract stevedores were used at other Bay Area Navy facilities but not at Port Chicago and Mare Island.) This debate over safety of procedures threaded through the court of inquiry, with each side attempting to pin the blame on the other.

The question of Captain Kinne's tonnage-figures blackboard and the competition it encouraged also came up during the proceedings. Kinne attempted to justify this practice as simply an extension of the Navy's practice of competition in target practice. He contended that it did not negatively impact on safety, and implied that junior officers who said it did, did not know what they were talking about.

While the officers scrambled unceremoniously to evade responsibility for the disaster, it became obvious that the matter of safety could not be ignored. In the following months the Navy tightened up its safety procedures concerning ammunition handling and upgraded the training for enlisted men and officers who were assigned this hazardous work. The loss of 320 lives was a high price to pay to learn the importance of safety and proper training—but before it was all over, the cost in human suffering would go still higher.

The court also heard testimony concerning the fueling of the vessels, possible sabotage, defects in the bombs, problems with the winches and other equipment, rough handling by the enlisted men, and organizational problems at Port Chicago. But the specific cause of the explosion was never established by the court of inquiry—anyone in a position to have actually seen what caused the explosion did not live to tell about it.

Nevertheless, the court was charged with offering an opinion on the cause of the explosion, and something or someone had to be held responsible for the awful tragedy. In his summation of the testimony the judge advocate dismissed sabotage as a possible cause on the grounds that an investigation by the District Intelligence Office had failed to turn up any evidence of sabotage. Inherent defects in the bombs might have been a "contributory cause," he said, "but there must have been some overt act to cause the bomb to actually explode." As for equipment problems and procedures employed, the judge advocate said the testimony was inconclusive: some witnesses testified that the equipment and methods used at Port Chicago were as safe as those employed at other naval magazines; other witnesses disagreed.

This brought the judge advocate to the question of the role of the black enlisted personnel:

> The consensus of opinion of the witnesses—and practically admitted by the interested parties—is that the col-

ored enlisted personnel are neither temperamentally or intellectually capable of handling high explosives. As one witness has stated, sixty percent of the lowest intellectual strata of the men sent out of Great Lakes were sent to Port Chicago. These men, it is testified, could not understand the orders which were given to them and the only way they could be made to understand what they should do was by actual demonstration. . . . It is an admitted fact, supported by the testimony of the witnesses, that there was rough and careless handling of the explosives being loaded aboard ships at Port Chicago.

In his summation the judge advocate could not avoid at least briefly noting the organizational problems that existed at Port Chicago and the absence of a Coast Guard loading detail the night of the explosion—these matters deserved some consideration by the court, he said. But he left no doubt as to where he thought the blame lay.

In its findings the court, for the most part, accepted the analysis of the judge advocate. The court listed the likely causes of the initial explosion in the order of probability as follows:

a. Presence of a supersensitive element which was detonated in the course of handling.

b. Rough handling by an individual or individuals. This may have occurred at any stage of the loading process from the breaking out of the cars to final stowage in the holds.

c. Failure of handling gear, such as the falling of a boom, failure of a block or hook, parting of a whip, etc.

d. Collision of the switch engine with an explosive loaded car, probably in the process of unloading.

e. An accident incident to the carrying away of the mooring lines of the *Quinalt Victory* or the bollards to which the *Quinalt Victory* was moored, resulting in damage to an explosive component.

f. The result of an act of sabotage. Although there is no evidence to support sabotage as a probable cause, it cannot be ignored as a possibility.

Although there was testimony before the court about competition in loading, this was not listed by the court (or the judge advocate) as in any way a cause of the explosion, although the court saw fit to recommend that in future "the loading of explosives should never be a matter of competition"—a small slap on the hands of the officers.

Thus, the court of inquiry in effect cleared the officers of responsibility for the disaster, and insofar as any human cause was invoked, the burden of blame was laid on the shoulders of the black enlisted men who died in the explosion.

MEN IN SHOCK

After the explosion many of the surviving black sailors were transferred to nearby Camp Shoemaker, where they remained until July 31; then the Fourth and Eighth Divisions were transferred to naval barracks in Vallejo, near Mare Island. During this period the men were assigned barracks duties but no shiploading. Another group, the Second Division, which was also at Camp Shoemaker until the 31st, returned to Port Chicago to help with the cleaning up and rebuilding of the base.

Many of the men were in a state of shock, troubled by the vivid memory of the horrible explosion in which so many of their friends had died. All were extremely nervous and jumpy. "Everybody was scared," one survivor recalled. "If somebody dropped a box or slammed a door, people began jumping around like crazy. Everybody was still nervous." Seaman Alvin Williams, who arrived at Port Chicago the day of the explosion, wrote home to his family: "It was something I'll never forget. I am in a pretty nervous condition now. Every loud noise I hear makes me jump and my heart flutters."

One man was not above exploiting the tension for the sake of a laugh. "He was a practical joker," Joe Small recalled. "We had large Honeywell heaters in the barracks, one at each end. He would come in at three in the morning. There was a big fan behind the heater. He would stick a newspaper in the fan to make a sudden

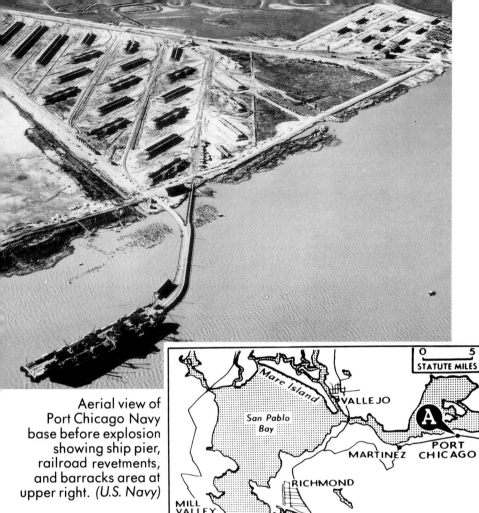

Aerial view of Port Chicago Navy base before explosion showing ship pier, railroad revetments, and barracks area at upper right. *(U.S. Navy)*

Map of San Francisco Bay Area. The **A** in upper right corner marks site of Port Chicago explosion. *(San Francisco Examiner)*

Black enlisted men unloading
ammunition from boxcar
under supervision of
white officer at Port Chicago.
Man bending over boxes is
Percy Robinson.
(Inset: Robinson today.)
(Photos courtesy Percy Robinson)

Joe Small, July 1946.

Joe Small, 1982.
(New York Daily News)

View of wreckage on shore as crane begins removing debris. *(U.S. Navy)*

View of wrecked pier. Submerged Stern of *Quinalt Victory* is at upper right.
(U.S. Navy)

Wreckage of *Quinalt Victory*. Note propeller from submerged stern. *(U.S. Navy)*

Aerial view showing destroyed pier and oil slick from *Quinalt Victory*. *(U.S. Navy)*

Barracks building after explosion. Barracks were located a mile from site of the blast. *(U.S. Navy)*

Wrecked recreation building. *(U.S. Navy)*

Interior of chow hall. *(U.S. Navy)*

Wrecked barracks buildings. *(U.S. Navy)*

Boxcars in protective revetments crushed by shock wave from blast.
(U.S. Navy)

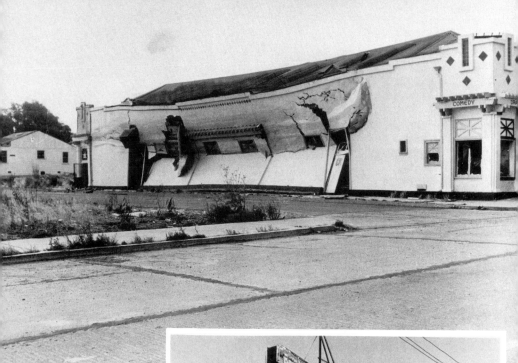

Port Chicago Theatre showing buckled wall after explosion. *(San Francisco Examiner)*

Joe Meyers, owner, in front of rebuilt Port Chicago Theatre in 1960s. *(Oakland Tribune)*

Captain Oscar Anderson, skipper of the *Redline*, examines unexploded 16-inch shell that crashed into ship's engine room when Port Chicago blew up. *(San Francisco Examiner)*

Rescue workers go about grim business of collecting remains of those killed in explosion. *(San Francisco Examiner)*

Port Chicago citizen who suffered eye injury in explosion. *(Oakland Tribune)*

First aid station in town of Port Chicago. *(Oakland Tribune)*

Interior of Port Chicago café day after explosion. *(Oakland Tribune)*

Port Chicago street scene day after blast. *(Oakland Tribune)*

Memorial assembly for Port Chicago victims, July 31, 1944. (*Oakland Tribune*)

Admiral Carleton Wright presents awards for bravery to officers and enlisted men who fought boxcar fire after explosion. (*Oakland Tribune*)

Seated around the table in front of the fifty accused seamen are the Navy officers who conducted the men's defense at the Treasure Island court-martial trial.

James Frank Coakley, prosecutor in mutiny trial.
(*San Francisco Examiner*)

Thurgood Marshall, special counsel for the NAACP, who handled appeal in mutiny case. (*San Francisco Examiner*)

A crane was brought in to help remove debris near pier. *(Oakland Tribune)*

Navy Seabees removing wrecked structure. *(Oakland Tribune)*

View of rebuilt Port Chicago pier in November 1944. *(U.S. Navy)*

Anti-Navy graffiti on fence outside Port Chicago home in 1967.
(Oakland Tribune)

Abandoned street and stray cow, all that remained after Port Chicago
was razed by the Navy in 1968. *(Oakland Tribune)*

Protest demonstration at Concord Naval Weapons Station (Port Chicago) in 1974. Note demonstrator holding newspaper reporting 1944 explosion.
(San Francisco Examiner)

Protest demonstration at Concord Naval Weapons Station (Port Chicago) in June 1987. The following month a demonstrator, Brian Willson, was gravely injured when a munitions train entering the base ran over him.
(San Francisco Examiner)

noise and then laugh when the men would bust out of their bunks and rush to the door. This was immediately after the explosion. He would stand there and laugh. Or he would suddenly turn on all the lights and holler 'Fire!' I mean this was all a joke to him. One night he really upset me. We had an ironing board sitting near the heater with a sheet over it to iron on. I lay in my bunk and watched him slide that sheet off and guide it until it got caught in the fan. He jumped back behind the heater. There was, I think, thirty-eight men in the barracks and all of them headed for that door at the same time. And several of them got hurt pretty bad. And he's standing there laughing. So that next morning I requested that he be moved out of our barracks. They moved him out."

The men's anxiety was made worse by the fact that they did not know what caused the explosion. Rumor and speculation were rife. Some thought it was caused by an accident, some suspected sabotage, others did not know what to think. Apparently the men were not informed that the Navy was conducting an investigation— certainly none of those who would later be involved in the work stoppage were called to testify at the court of inquiry. Thus the men attempted to evaluate their situation in the absence of any definite information, and quite naturally their conversations focused on the ammunition and the work process itself. It was no longer possible to blithely discount the risks of ammunition handling. "They assured me that it couldn't happen," Small reflected. "Without that detonator and the cap, it was supposed to be innocent. It couldn't explode. I don't know what caused the initial explosion but that so-called innocent ammunition is what did most of the damage."

Another survivor said: "Put me on a ship and let me fight out there, take my chances there. Why lose your life on somebody else's negligence?"

Given the conditions under which the men worked, the question that loomed ever larger was: If it happened once, what was to prevent it from happening again? To this no satisfactory answer was ever offered.

The men talked among themselves. They had not yet been ordered back to their regular duty and no one knew what would happen next, but many of them hoped they would be transferred to other stations or to ships. One man asked his lieutenant for a transfer to overseas duty, thinking to himself: "Man, I got a chance

over there with the enemy, but I ain't got no chance in that hold."
This was the same individual who recalled how before the explosion
the men sometimes joked about who would be first out of the hold
in case of trouble. Now joking did not help; the reality was too
awful.

Many of the survivors expected to be granted survivors' leaves
to visit their families before being reassigned to regular duty. But
such leaves were not granted, creating a major grievance—and one
which could not be balanced by the rapidly diminishing benefits
of Navy life. A survivor recalled what happened: "When we got
back together before we had to go back to work, I think the talk
was about going home—we're all talking about going home. We
thought we were entitled to go home. So we just decided that if
they wouldn't let us go home, we wasn't going to work." Then he
added: "I guess all your little grievances come out that built up
long before. A lot of things you didn't like before, you just didn't
do anything about them. But now they're all piled up."

Another man who worked on the cleanup crew said: "This is
what made the guys mad after they done that work around there
getting things straightened out and then they turned them down.
They said, 'No, you cannot have that thirty-day leave.'"

Even men who had been hospitalized with injuries were not
granted leaves.

CHAPTER

6

The Work Stoppage

The Fourth and Eighth Divisions were transferred to the Ryder Street Naval Barracks in Vallejo on July 31. The barracks were located near the foot of Sonoma Street; across the Napa River was an ammunition loading depot on the south end of Mare Island.

Some of the enlisted men were already talking among themselves about whether they would go back to work loading ammunition. Indeed, with the transfer to Vallejo the men suspected that they were going to be loading ammunition at the Mare Island Ammunition Depot. It was now clear that there would be no transfer to other work, as some had hoped; there would be no thirty-day survivors' leaves; the men were going to be sent back to loading ammunition under the same officers as before.

Fearful of another explosion, angry at the treatment accorded them, the men began talking of not going back to work. For many the risk of another explosion was uppermost in their minds. One survivor recalled: "We didn't want no more loading ammunition because of what happened at Port Chicago. No more loading anywhere." Some felt that even combat duty was less risky. At least there was a chance of survival; in the hold of a ship there was no chance if an explosion occurred. Other men were not only con-

75

cerned about the risks—they now found their treatment by the Navy not only unjust but intolerable. One man recalled his attitude: "I just said: No, I ain't going back on that damn thing [shiploading]. Why don't they get some whiteys and put them down there. I said hell, I'm a gunneryman. They taught me how to fire guns; I'm supposed to be on a ship. Now they got me working as a stevedore. And I'm not getting stevedore's pay."

Several men recalled the denial of survivors' leaves as a particular source of dissatisfaction and anger. One survivor said the men were talking about "how they didn't want to go back to work under those conditions because they hadn't treated us right, see, and that they were letting them white boys go home for thirty-day leaves and we wasn't getting nothing."

Joe Small and some other men linked the cause of the explosion to the working conditions on the pier. For them the thought of returning to the same working conditions—competition, rushing, etc.—under the same officers was intolerable. "I was a winch operator on the ship," recounted Small, "and I missed killing a man on the average of once a day—killing or permanently injuring a man. And it was all because of rushing, speed. I didn't want to go back into this. This was my reason for refusing to go back to work—to get the working conditions changed. I realized that I had to work. I wasn't trying to shirk work. I don't think these other men were trying to shirk work. But to go back to work under the same conditions, with no improvements, no changes, the same group of officers that we had, was just—we thought there was a better alternative, that's all."

At some point several men approached Small, who, as a kind of informal leader, was generally respected by the others. They asked him what he intended to do. Small made it plain that he did not intend to go back to loading ammunition. Some also approached another man who was considered knowledgeable, with the same question. He responded that he didn't care what anyone else did, but he wasn't going back to loading. Other men also expressed their opposition to returning to loading ammunition. Gradually the notion of a collective work stoppage began to take shape. Indeed, some in the group came to believe that if all or the overwhelming majority of the enlisted men refused to handle ammunition, then the Navy would be compelled to change the working conditions or transfer the men to other work.

Significantly, not everyone who was to join the work stoppage participated in these early discussions. Martin Bordenave was injured in the explosion and hospitalized for some days afterward. By the time he was released he had already decided not to return to work: "I didn't talk to nobody. I didn't conspire with nobody. I just made up my mind I was tired of it. I wanted to be a sailor."

Someone came up with the idea of drawing up a petition, a list of all the men who were unwilling to continue handling ammunition and wanted a transfer of duty. Some fifty or sixty men signed the petition; others refused to sign; and still others felt the petition was useless. When it got to him, Joe Small thought the petition was a bad idea and he destroyed it. Later he explained his action to me: "Well, I knew—I guess mostly from instinct—that anything in writing is more damaging to you than a verbal conversation. And when you put your name on a list, then you become a supporting part of whatever that list stands for. And there's very little chance of your changing your mind even if you wanted to."

Small was also aware that some kind of letter of protest had been sent out by Port Chicago men in 1943 and apparently nothing had come of it. Small was convinced that he and the other men were justified in not going back to work. "I knew that situation under which we worked hadn't been changed. I had made up my mind that I wasn't going back to work under these conditions."

Small's response was characteristic of him. That he emerged as a leader was due to a combination of opportune circumstance and feisty character. Small was not a man who shrank from acting. Nor did he lightly tolerate what he regarded as abuse. At age sixteen he settled accounts with a white boy who taunted him. "He had been calling me 'Smoky.' Every time he did it he would run and hide behind his cousin who was six feet two and weighed over two hundred pounds. I promised that one day I would catch him when his cousin wasn't there. The opportunity didn't present itself until we returned to school in September 1937. He called me 'Smoky' and his big cousin wasn't with him. I put a good whipping on him. They gave me an alternative: either to leave school or be sent to a reform school. So I left school. That ended my formal education."

For a time Small helped his mother run the farm, but then in July 1939 he enrolled in the Civilian Conservation Corps and was soon promoted to lieutenant. Pugnacious though he was, Small could also calm down hotheads and stop a fight. That's how he became a lieutenant. "I was one of the men cutting brush in the woods with an axe. Two fellas got in an argument, and they had brush axes. I stepped between them and stopped the argument, and asked them both for the brush axes. 'You give me your axe, and you give me your axe.' And that stopped the fight. Well, then the men began to respect me, to look up to me. One of the officers called me one day and said, 'Small, you have a natural leadership ability. I'm going to make you a lieutenant.' "

Joe Small was equally audacious with machines. That's how he learned to drive a tractor-trailer. "A fella came along the highway one day in a tractor-trailer, and he had a load of logs. He had telephone poles, but they were debarked. He stopped for a cup of coffee, and I was admiring the load of logs he had on the truck. It was an International, an old International. He said, 'You think you can move that?' And I said, 'Sure, I can move that. I can drive anything on wheels.' I'd never driven anything 'cept a tractor on the farm. So he said, 'The key's in it. Go ahead.' So I got up in it. Well, I had learned the standard shift from my brother who had an old Essex, a car, and I knew where first, second, high, and reverse was. I just took a chance that the truck would be the same way. I got it in gear and moved it off, drove.

"It was rolling along, and the guy yelled. I hit the brakes, but I didn't know they were air brakes. Air brakes was a brand-new thing. It stopped on a dime, and a log came through the back window and went out through the front windshield, right past my head.

"The guy was hot about it; he did a bit of cussing. But I didn't allow him to get within reach of me. I finally walked off and left him with his truck, swearing, jumping up and down. That was my first encounter with a tractor-trailer. From then on, every time I got a chance to climb into one, I climbed into it and moved it."

Small picked up several truck-driving jobs, and he quickly learned to operate other kinds of equipment, including cranes, backhoes, and bulldozers. He attributes his aptitude with machinery to the influence of his father. In addition to being a farmer and a preacher, the elder Small also did carpentry and welding, and he repaired all of his farm machinery himself. It was not surprising that young Small gained the confidence to jump into a tractor-trailer and try to drive it. He was driving a truck for a flour company in New

Brunswick, New Jersey, earning thirty dollars a week, when he was drafted in 1943.

At Port Chicago, Small felt that leadership was thrust upon him. It began with him being selected cadence caller. "I remember one day we had a petty officer calling cadence. We were on the drill field, and they had to separate some of the men. Somebody said, 'Small can call cadence,' and that's where it started. I had about three men, I think, and we were marching up and down the drill field. And then a couple of days later the petty officer was late getting back or something like that, and they asked me to call cadence. I was in the ranks calling cadence and then somebody said, 'I can't hear him, let him get outside.' I stepped outside the ranks and from then on I was the official cadence caller for the division. I could have refused it, but I rather enjoyed marching outside of the ranks and calling cadence."

Leadership may have been thrust upon Small, but he also welcomed and enjoyed it. When the anonymous voice of chance spoke, Small was ready to answer and act.

Gradually, Small assumed more of the duties of the petty officers. "I was always an early riser, I was always the first one up in the morning. It became my expected job to wake the men up and get them out of there." Increasingly the men came to Small when they had problems rather than going to the petty officers. And officers used Small as a go-between: "They used to call me from the quarterdeck, in place of the petty officers, if there was some business to transact with the division. It was thrust on me because—well, without sounding silly—I had the ability. They recognized it, but they wouldn't give me the rank. My lieutenant said I was too young to be a petty officer."

Small's curiosity about the mechanics of shiploading, and his irrepressible gumption, got him one of the better and more responsible jobs at Port Chicago. Shortly after he arrived he began to watch the winch operators who controlled the cables and booms and nets that lifted cargo from the pier into the ships' holds. He was fascinated, and he sometimes slipped away during the lunch break to study and manipulate the levers on one of these machines. An opportunity to demonstrate his new skill soon presented itself: "Down on the ship I was one of the dock hands. They had four winches in operation and they had five winchmen; one winchman was relief. Whenever a winchman wanted to leave his post, then they had a replacement there to take over for him for ten minutes. So, a fella had to leave on an emergency, and he just walked off from the winch. He just dropped it and walked away. And somebody said, 'Hey! Where's that winchman?' I had been playing around with the winch; during our break at lunchtime I'd go up and play with it. I said, 'I'll run it while he's gone.' I went up and took over. It was a steam one; it was very difficult to operate, in that the positions was very ticklish—not like an electric winch. I operated it to the satisfaction of the lieutenant, so whenever they needed a replacement or relief man, they called on me, and eventually I took over the job completely."

Small also developed a reputation as a man who would stand up to the officers on behalf of the enlisted men. For example, in the weeks before the disaster it was Small who confronted the officers about the danger of an explosion because of the way the men had to rush. Small was certainly outspoken, and he would eventually come to think of himself as a "spokesman" for the work refusers; the officers would label him the "ringleader" of a mutiny.

THE WORK STOPPAGE

The idea of a work stoppage was a desperate gamble, and from the beginning there were problems. In the first place there was no definite plan of action. Moreover, not everyone was willing to go along with the work stoppage: some men, fearing punishment, were willing to go back to work. As events moved along, attempts to convince everyone to stick together and maintain the unity essential to their hoped-for success sometimes led to arguments and fights. Each man had to decide whether he would be loyal to the group in its resistance, or whether he would disavow the resistance and return to work. This was obviously an emotionally charged time as the men talked and argued among themselves and considered what to do. Many men simply felt confused, and it was not possible to say what would happen until the men were presented with an actual choice. As it turned out, each man had to decide not once but several times what he would do.

The first choices had to be made on August 9, three weeks after the Port Chicago explosion. Earlier that week work gloves were distributed to the men of the Fourth Division. Someone quipped, "If these are for handling ammunition, chief, I never touch the stuff," but all the men took the gloves. A ship, the U.S.S. *San Gay*, had arrived at Mare Island to be loaded with ammunition. The Fourth, Eighth, and Second Divisions were scheduled to load. After chow on the 9th the Fourth Division men were ordered to fall in for work. Joe Small assisted the petty officers in taking muster, then the division was ordered to march off. The men still did not know for certain where they were going, but they did know that at a certain juncture in the road they could be ordered to turn right, which would take them to the parade ground, or they could be ordered to turn left, which would take them to a ferry that crossed the river to the ammunition loading dock. Small, who was calling cadence, described what happened next:

"I was marching on the left-hand side of the ranks. When the lieutenant gave the command, 'Column left,' everybody stopped dead, boom, just like that. He said, 'Forward, march—column left!' Nobody moved.

"Later an officer got up on a platform at the parade ground and said, 'Small, front and center.' I walked up and crossed to the front, stopped in front of him. He said, 'Small, are you going back to work?' And I told him, 'No, sir.' He asked why. I said I was afraid. Then somebody over in the ranks said, 'If Small don't go, we're not going, either.' Well, that put me in the forefront of everything, made me the spokesman for the whole group."

Lieutenant Delucchi went to the administration building to report the matter to his superiors. The base chaplain, Lieutenant Commander Jefferson Flowers, then came over to talk to the men: "I told them I wanted to talk to them and to gather there around me. They came forward and gathered around me, and I asked them what the trouble was, and they said they didn't want to go over and load ammunition or handle ammunition. I tried to persuade them that it was their duty to do so. They still persisted, saying they would not handle ammunition. Then I appealed to their race pride and mentioned the fact that they were letting down the loyal men of their race and their friends as well, if they didn't, and all to no avail; they still said that they would obey any other order but they would not handle ammunition, that they were afraid to do so."

When Chaplain Flowers's efforts to shame the men into returning to work by appealing to race pride and patriotism did not succeed, he and some of the officers offered to share the risk by being present while the men worked. The chaplain, for example, told the men that he was also afraid of ammunition but that he would go with them if they would go. But the men were skeptical. As one of them recounted: "We knew that they weren't going to stay there with us. All the officers, they get you down there and then as soon as you start working, they're gone." The men's response to the chaplain was to ask if they were not entitled to survivors' leaves.

The Fourth Division men were then ordered to the recreation building, where they would be interviewed one by one about their willingness to work and told they could face severe penalties. Some agreed to return to work; most did not. However, the interviews were interrupted before all men were talked to.

Meanwhile, the officers of the Second and Eighth Port Chicago Divisions were instructed to order their men to work. It was not certain whether the men were given direct orders or were simply asked if they were willing to work. In any case, most of these men balked. This process took up most of the afternoon.

The men who continued to express an unwillingness to handle ammunition were confined to a barge tied to a pier until the officers could decide what to do. Of 328 men in the three divisions, 258 were imprisoned on the barge. Meanwhile, civilian contract stevedores were hurriedly recruited to load the *San Gay*.

THE BARGE MEETING

Like captives in the hold of a slave ship, the men were confined to the cramped quarters of the barge for three days. Tensions were high. Officers had told the men they faced serious charges. There were also conflicts with the guards, and some of the enlisted men assembled makeshift weapons to defend themselves. Others wanted to forget about the resistance and go back to work. Small recalled an encounter with one such man. "He was a little fellow, young, about seventeen years old. He wanted to go back to work, and he asked me could he leave the barge to go back to work. I told him, 'You can, but I wouldn't advise it.' I advised him to stay with the men and we'd all see this through together. If we go back as a unit, then that's one thing. But if we go back one at a time, the one that goes back will be looked down on by the others as a traitor and a deserter."

Evidently the young man took Small's cagey advice to heart.

Everyone was on edge. Men were angry and fearful, and almost in a state of panic. Arguments were frequent, and more than one fight broke out as men disagreed over whether they should return to work.

As it turned out, going back to work was really no longer an option. One group of men contacted their division officer and told him they were willing to go back to work. The officer told them it was too late, and they were left on the barge.

The men were marched from the barge to the chow hall for meals. On August 10 a fight broke out in the chow hall. The men were not permitted to smoke on the barge or in the chow hall, but apparently someone started to smoke and this led to a fight with one of the guards. The fight was broken up, but maintaining the unity and discipline of the group was proving more and more difficult.

That evening Joe Small and some of the other enlisted men who had been assigned to keep order on the barge discussed the growing tension among the men. It was agreed to call a meeting of all the men. Small later recalled the situation: "There was a general state of rebellion on the barge. That's why I called the meeting. The men were arming themselves with homemade knives, spoons that were turned into knives, things like that. It was a pretty hairy situation and I got into it to try to offset a disaster that I saw coming, which was some of the men getting shot or some of the marines getting hurt. If a marine had come on that barge and the men decided to do something to him, there was no escape for him. By the same token, if they started shooting on that barge, there's no way possible to hit any one particular man because we were too packed on there. And fights had broken out over differences of opinion. Two men would get to fighting right there on the barge because one thought that he should go back to duty and another thought he shouldn't. And if five men got to fighting on that barge, ten or twelve could get killed. That's how densely packed we were. And as long as there was division on the barge there was a chance of a riot. So it was in my interest, being one of those imprisoned on that barge, it was in my interest to offset any violence that might occur. I thought about calling a meeting and talking to the men to quell their anger a little, cool them down. This is what I was attempting to do."

Small called the meeting and spoke to the men. He urged the men to "knock off the horseplay" and obey the guards. He stressed that the men should avoid getting into trouble. "That is just what the officers want us to do; they want us to mess up. The officers want us to do something so they can mess us up, so they will have something on us. If we obey the shore patrol and the officers and don't get into any trouble, they can't do anything to us. If we do get into trouble, they are liable to call in the marines." Then he told the men: "We've got the officers by the balls—they can do nothing to us if we don't do anything to them. If we stick together, they can't do anything to us."

The meeting lasted only a few minutes. It seemed to have the desired effect; some of the men applauded when Small finished speaking. Whatever may have been Small's motives, the fact that a meeting took place on the barge later became known to the officers (some of the men suspected there was a snitch in their group), and during the mutiny trial the fact of the meeting was presented by the prosecution as evidence that Small had organized a mutinous conspiracy among the men.

If Small was organizing, "mutinous conspiracies" were hardly his only concern. According to another enlisted man, Small also organized the men to handle their meals and to minimize problems in the chow hall. Some men cooked, others served, and others cleaned the kitchen. The level heads among the men were anxious to encourage cooperation and to show the officers that the men were willing to obey all orders except to load ammunition. "In other words, what we was doing, we was avoiding trouble," one man recalled. "We was setting up a system where they couldn't say, 'Heck, they don't want to do nothing.' Anything they wanted done, we did it."

The men were still uncertain as to what their fate would be. The optimists thought that if they stuck together they might be transferred to other duty, or given dishonorable discharges. Some thought they might be imprisoned for a while. No one expected they would be charged with mutiny. "We didn't even know what mutiny meant," one man recounted. "We thought mutiny was something like when you kill people or take over something. We didn't know you could define disobeying orders as being mutiny. We thought mutiny could only happen on a ship."

"As far as we were concerned mutiny could only be committed on the high seas," Small would later say. "And we weren't on the high seas. I, for one, didn't consider refusing to go to work mutiny. We didn't try to take over anything. We didn't try to take command of the base. We didn't try to replace any officers; we didn't try to assume an officer's position. How could they call it mutiny?"

But call it mutiny they did.

SELECTING THE FIFTY "MUTINEERS"

The following day, August 11, the men from the barge were marched to the baseball diamond and assembled in a U-formation, under heavily armed guard. Shortly, Admiral Wright arrived in a jeep and addressed the men. One of them recalled the admiral's words: "Just in case you don't know who I am, my name is Admiral Wright and I am the commandant of the Twelfth Naval District. They tell me that some of you men want to go to sea. I believe that's a goddamn lie! I don't believe any of you have enough guts to go to sea. I handled ammunition for approximately thirty years and I'm still here. I have a healthy respect for ammunition; anybody who doesn't is crazy. But I want to remind you men that mutinous conduct in time of war carries the death sentence, and the hazards of facing a firing squad are far greater than the hazards of handling ammunition."

The death threat made by the admiral came as a shock to the men. Most were stunned, but some couldn't believe it and tried to discount the threat. One man muttered: "Man, this guy can't have nobody shot! We ain't fighting no war here. They can't do this. They'd have to have an Act of Congress to shoot somebody in the United States." But this thin hope could not be sustained.

Admiral Wright dramatically raised the stakes in the confrontation. The risks of continued resistance had been made painfully evident and could no longer be discounted. The choice between returning to ammunition work or continuing to refuse appeared now to be a choice between possible death and certain death. It was a terrible dilemma, and emotional tensions reached their highest level as the men considered their awful options.

The admiral spoke briefly with some of the men individually, then departed. After the admiral left, the men were ordered by their division officers to fall into two groups—those willing to obey all orders and those not willing. It was an incredibly difficult moment: several men wept openly as they chose one side or the other; two brothers separated and took opposite positions; many men vacillated, going first to one group, then to the other. Some men protested that they were still afraid of ammunition, and they were assigned to the unwilling group. With gallows humor another man teased his partner: "What you gonna do? You gonna let them shoot you blindfolded or you gonna be looking at them!"

In the end, all of the Eighth Division indicated their willingness to work and all but forty-four men in the other two divisions found themselves in the willing group. The forty-four refusers were taken away under guard. The next day they were joined by six other men from the Second and Fourth Divisions who had indicated they were willing to work but who failed to show up for work duty.

Among the fifty men were some of those whom the officers considered the "ringleaders" of the mutiny, such as Joe Small. However, some men who actively encouraged others not to work (for example, by circulating petitions) were not in the group of fifty—at the last moment they agreed to go back to work, creating much ill will among those whom they had recruited to resist. Joe Small described the fifty as "loudmouths and fighters," the "most nervy men" who stood up for themselves. But this description did not accurately characterize the group, either.

Some of the fifty were certainly men who refused to be cowed by the officers. Others may simply have had the misfortune to be disliked by their division officers for other reasons and therefore found themselves among the "mutineers." For example, two men were permanently assigned as mess cooks—one because he had a nervous condition that made him a hazard to others on the pier, the other because he was underweight. Yet these two were now ordered to load ammunition, and when they hesitated, they were thrown in with the mutineers. Another man had fractured his wrist in an accident on August 8, and even though his arm was in a cast, he too was ordered to work. When he protested he found himself placed with the mutineers. Thus, the fifty men were not necessarily "ringleaders," nor were they all "loudmouths and fighters." Some were simply victims of the whims of their commanding officers.

INTERROGATION

The fifty men were taken to the brig at Camp Shoemaker. Small was placed in solitary confinement while the others were interrogated. Meanwhile, the 208 men who were considered willing to work did not go back to work; instead, they were also brought to Camp Shoemaker for interrogation and summary court-martials. Thus all of the men were now faced with another hard choice: whether they would give evidence against each other during the ensuing investigation. The men were questioned without benefit of counsel; indeed several of them thought that the interrogators were their defense lawyers. The investigation continued through the month of August, and statements were obtained from almost all of the 258 men. Armed guards were present when at least some of the statements were taken, and it became a point of contention at the mutiny trial as to whether the statements were obtained voluntarily or under duress.

The interrogating officers were particularly anxious to gain evidence concerning the "ringleaders" of the alleged mutiny, especially Joe Small. Everyone was threatened with a general court-martial. One man recalled that as soon as he went in for questioning he was told that he could be sentenced to seven and a half to fifteen years. Then he was asked about the meeting on the prison barge —who spoke and what was said. He denied knowing about the meeting. Another man, a Southerner, described how the interrogators attempted to turn him against Small and another alleged leader by suggesting that since they were from the North and had some education, "they don't mean you no good." "What they wanted you to do," this man recalled, "they wanted you to hang numbers on Small." When asked by officers if Small was the leader, he answered no. "He said, 'Well, somebody has got to be the leader, everybody needs a leader.' I said nobody made me do nothing. I said we don't need a leader if you know what's going on on that base."

When direct questioning and threats didn't work, cajoling was tried. "I remember being interviewed by an officer that I knew from Port Chicago, who said he was my friend and all this kind of thing," Jack Crittenden recalled. "He said, 'Jack, I'm here to help you. You're in trouble and I'm here to help you.' I said, 'Yeah, it looks like I'm in trouble—I got a big "P" on me.' He said, 'Tell me what happened on the barge.' I said, 'Lieutenant, I don't know what went on on the barge. I was a scared jackrabbit on the barge.' He said, 'Now Jack, you know what went on on that barge.' Well, we had this fellow, X, let's call him, in our division—an unintelligent country boy who would try to please anyone, say anything they wanted, if they claimed to be his friend. X was questioned before me. So the lieutenant told me, 'Jack, you're not being very cooperative. X told me you spoke at the meeting, and that you were one of the guards.' 'Me?' I said, 'Not me. I was too scared to move. I thought certain that any minute the marines were gonna call me out and shoot me.' I'm just telling the lieutenant this because I know damn well that he wasn't my friend. He was wearing a uniform and he was a lieutenant in the Navy. I was wearing a 'P' and I was a prisoner. He wasn't there to help me. So I wasn't cooperative, I didn't say the things he wanted to hear. That made the marine guard so mad I thought he was going to beat me up when I came out of there."

In any case, with 258 men to question it was inevitable that some would identify Joe Small as having spoken at the barge meeting and name others as having encouraged the men not to return to work. For his part, Small never denied having spoken at the meeting, although at the trial he would deny having said things which, in fact, he did.

The interrogators drafted written statements based on what the men told them, and each man was called to sign such a statement. Some men balked, saying the statements were not their own words and did not accurately reflect what they had said. A few men refused to sign the statements, but most signed in the belief that they had no choice.

CHAPTER

7

The Mutiny Trial: Prosecution

Two days after the work stoppage Captain Goss sent a written report to Admiral Wright in which he described the "mutinous action" of the black sailors. Goss, who never hesitated to express his dislike for any signs of assertiveness among the black sailors under his command, claimed that the source of the problem was "agitators, ringleaders, among these men." How else could you explain the men's allegations of discrimination, especially given, in Goss's words, "the extreme care and patience which has been exercised at both Mare Island and Port Chicago to avoid discrimination"? Only a newfound "mutinous attitude" introduced by "outside propaganda and subversive influence" could explain this behavior.

Wright forwarded Goss's report to Washington, gratuitously adding his own opinion that "a considerable portion of the men involved are of a low order of mentality. . . ." Wright, however, realized that some action must be taken to defuse the appearance of racial discrimination. He recommended introduction of a personnel rotation system in which black enlistees at Mare Island and Port Chicago would "not be retained indefinitely at those stations if they desire other duty for which they are suitable." Further, he was given authority by the Navy's Bureau of Personnel to have one unit of white enlisted men sent to work at Port Chicago and one at Mare Island. This proposal to allow some blacks to rotate out while bringing in two white units gave the appearance of change without seriously challenging segregation. There was no integration of units proposed, nor any suggestion of integrating the officers' ranks. The plan quickly gained approval.

A 1912 graduate of Annapolis, Carleton Wright had served on a destroyer in World War I. Between the wars he held posts at various stations as gunnery and ordnance officer. He was awarded a Navy Cross while a commander of a task force that engaged Japanese warships in 1942. Returning to the United States, he was appointed commandant of the Twelfth Naval District in January 1944.

Wright, who had actually spoken with some of the rebellious men when he went to Mare Island, observed that "the refusal to perform the required work arises from a mass fear arising out of the Port Chicago explosion." Yet the admiral recommended that the 208 men who balked be given summary court-martials on charges of refusing to obey orders, while the fifty who "continued to override authority" would be charged with mutiny. Implicit in the admiral's report, ironically, were issues that would surface later at the trial. If the men were motivated by "mass fear," then this could explain their behavior without invoking a conspiracy. And if the 208 could be guilty of no more than refusing to obey orders, then where was the qualitative difference in the behavior of the fifty that would justify trying them on the much more serious charge of overriding military authority and making a mutiny?

On August 31 President Franklin D. Roosevelt was informed of the situation by Secretary of the Navy James V. Forrestal. Forrestal, formerly a Wall Street investment banker who joined the Roosevelt administration in 1940 and became Secretary of the Navy in 1944, sent a memo and attached copies of the reports by Goss and Wright. He repeated Wright's suggestion that it was "mass fear" that motivated the men's refusal to work. Forrestal also advised the President that in order "to avoid any semblance of discrimination against negroes [sic]," authorization had been procured to send white work units to Port Chicago and Mare Island.

Roosevelt reviewed the report and on September 2 sent a note to Forrestal. In the President's view the 208 men who balked should receive only nominal sentences because "they were acti-vated by mass fear and . . . this was understandable." He said nothing about the fifty accused of mutiny, although Wright's com-ment about fear was with reference to the original 258. With the President's brief note the die was cast.

Significantly, in a move that tells much about the political re-lationship between Roosevelt and his wife, the President passed the Secretary's report along to Eleanor Roosevelt, "for your infor-mation," as he wrote her, undoubtedly knowing that liberal activist Eleanor might well take some contrary action. Eleanor Roosevelt felt a strong identification with racially oppressed people, although she tended to see their protests as motivated by feelings of infe-riority. She sided with Walter White, head of the NAACP, when he strongly protested the Senate filibuster of an antilynching bill in 1935. "If I were colored," she wrote, "I think I should have about the same obsession that he has." Then she mused: "The type of thing which would make him get himself arrested in the Senate restaurant is probably an inferiority complex which he tries to combat and which makes him far more aggressive than if he felt equality. . . ." Poor Walter White! That he might be legitimately angered by continued government ineffectuality against lynching seemingly did not occur to the First Lady. Yet, if Eleanor Roo-sevelt's psychological ruminations were not endearing, her well-known activism against racial discrimination made her an important public ally for groups like the NAACP. And from the President's viewpoint the activities of the First Lady did not hurt his support among minority voters, quite the contrary.

The President's administration, on the other hand, generally took an interest in racial matters only when they could not be avoided, as in the case of A. Philip Randolph's threatened march on Wash-ington in 1941, or when some situation might provoke an adverse reaction among the black electorate. Black voters solidly supported Roosevelt in 1936 but were more equivocal in 1940, showing cracks in the New Deal coalition. In 1944 Roosevelt enjoyed great support among blacks, with the legendary Mary McLeod Bethune orga-nizing a National Non-Partisan Committee for the Re-election of Roosevelt. But black support could not be taken for granted, and in fact the nationally circulated and influential *Pittsburgh Courier*, with several hundred thousand black readers, would come out for Thomas Dewey. Hence the growing sensitivity to the racial issue as the memos on the rebellion at Mare Island percolated up through the military chain of command and into the offices of the administration. To both the military commanders and the administration the rotation of blacks and whites at Mare Island and Port Chicago seemed a sufficient response to the discrimination issue. Eleanor Roosevelt's response would reveal itself later.

In early September 1944 Admiral Wright formally charged the fifty men with conspiring to make a mutiny. The specification of the charge was that they, "having conspired each with the other to mutiny against the lawful authority of their superior naval officers duly set over them, by refusing to work in the operation of loading ammunition aboard ships and unloading ammunition from ships, did, on or about 11 August 1944, at said Naval Barracks, make a mutiny . . . in that they . . . did then and there wilfully, concertedly and persistently disobey, disregard and defy [a] lawful order [to work] with a deliberate purpose and intent to override superior military authority; the United States then being in a state of war."

The last clause, "the United States then being in a state of war," was critical because any sailors convicted of mutiny during wartime could be sentenced to the maximum punishment—death. In any case, if convicted, the men faced prison terms of fifteen years if not death. The prospects were decidedly grim.

A seven-member court was appointed by Admiral Wright to hear the evidence and decide a verdict in the case. The court, composed of senior naval officers, was headed by Rear Admiral Hugo W. Osterhaus, a forty-year career officer brought out of retirement for the occasion. The prosecution team was headed by Lieutenant Commander James F. Coakley. Coakley had been assistant to Earl Warren when Warren was the district attorney of Alameda County, the county in which the city of Oakland is located. He served as deputy chief prosecutor in Warren's office. After the war Coakley would be elected district attorney of Alameda County, a post he would hold for many years, gaining notoriety in the 1960s as the hard-line DA who prosecuted antiwar activists and Black Panthers. Coakley was assisted as judge advocate by Lieutenant (j.g.) John T. Keenan. The judge advocate's office also provided a legal team for the defendants headed by Lieutenant Gerald E. Veltmann, a Texan who had been an attorney in civilian life. The defendants were divided into groups of ten and each assigned a defense lawyer. Other members of the defense included Lieutenants (j.g.) Irving J.

Hayutin, Daniel F. Hanley, Phillip J. Hermann, and Lieutenant Harley Carswell.

The trial opened on Thursday, September 14. The proceedings were held in a small wooden building that had once been a marine barracks, now converted into a courtroom for the occasion. Although the courtroom was unimpressive, its setting was not—for the trial was held at the naval installation on Yerba Buena Island, more popularly known as Treasure Island after the 1939–40 San Francisco Fair. Situated in almost the center of the bay, Treasure Island commands magnificent views of San Francisco and the Golden Gate Bridge to the west, and to the east, Oakland, Berkeley, and the east bay hills. North of Treasure Island were Richmond, Vallejo, and the huge naval base at Mare Island, located on San Pablo Bay, an extension of the San Francisco Bay into which the Sacramento River emptied. To the south were Santa Clara and San Jose. A rocky anchor for the Bay Bridge, Treasure Island was linked to both San Francisco and Oakland by it. All around the island the bay was bustling with civilian and military vessels of every description. Bay Area ports struggled to deal with an immense flow of troops, machines, and matériel as the United States prepared to retake the Philippine Islands and press on to Japan.

The courtroom was small and crowded. On one side, behind a curving table, sat the members of the court, the senior naval officers presided over by Rear Admiral Osterhaus, who would act as both judge and jury. Directly opposite were tables for the prosecution and defense attorneys. The fifty accused seamen sat with their backs against a wall, more on the periphery than at the heart of the scene.

Navy public relations officers gave the case much fanfare, handing out press statements and photographs of the trial. The court-martial was described as the first mutiny trial of World War II and the largest mass trial in the history of the Navy.* Unlike with other

---

*The most famous mass mutiny trial in U.S. history occurred in 1840 after fifty-three kidnaped Africans revolted against slavers on the vessel *Amistad* the year before. After wandering the high seas for many weeks the *Amistad* arrived in U.S. waters off Montauk Point. The thirty-eight surviving Africans were taken in custody and charged with mutiny and murder. When the Africans demanded their freedom on grounds that they had been kidnaped by outlaw slave traders (the slave trade having been prohibited in 1820), the case made headlines and antislavery forces rallied to the support of the Africans. The case went all the way to the U.S. Supreme Court where, in 1841, the Africans were acquitted. The court upheld the principle that persons escaping from illegal slavery had the right to use force to regain their freedom.

military trials, the press was encouraged to cover the mutiny court-martial, and several newspaper and wire service reporters filed stories from the proceedings every day. The Navy was anxious to have the trial publicized, perhaps to counter charges that it would be a kangaroo court and perhaps also to intimidate other dissident sailors. In any case prosecutor Coakley, the judge advocate, was confident that he had an airtight case against the fifty men.

THE PROSECUTION

Coakley had good reason to feel confident. Even before the trial opened, the defense had suffered a major defeat. In a pretrial brief Lieutenant Veltmann had sought to have the mutiny charge dismissed. Citing *Winthrop's Military Law and Precedents*, he noted that mutiny was defined as "unlawful opposition or resistance to, or defiance of, superior military authority with a deliberate purpose to usurp, subvert or override the same." Veltmann argued that the charge did not allege that the accused men conspired together or intended to seize command from their superior officers. Some may have disobeyed an order, but that was not mutiny. Coakley countered in a brief of his own that under military law "evidence showing a joint, collective and persistent refusal by two or more men in the military or naval service to work after a lawful order to do so, or what might be commonly called a 'strike' by a group of military or naval personnel, constitutes sufficient proof of a conspiracy to subvert or override superior military authority and consequently sufficient proof under the law of the charge of making a mutiny." The court, siding with Coakley's view, refused to dismiss the charge.

Overlooked in this preliminary skirmish was an alternative conception of what had happened at Mare Island—ironically suggested by the prosecution's brief—namely, that the men's actions constituted a strike, a work stoppage. A refusal to work is a passive act of resistance; there is no intent to seize power. A mutiny, on the other hand, is active revolt with the intent of taking charge. No doubt if the accused men had been civilian stevedores, their action would have been called a wildcat strike, and they would not be on trial for their lives. Coakley's casual equating of a strike with a mutiny unintentionally revealed his fundamental approach to the case—produce evidence to show a conspiracy to strike and this can be presented as equivalent to a conspiracy to mutiny. Conspiracy was the critical link.

In the meantime, Coakley disclosed to the press that the 208 men who had originally been refusers but then agreed to work had been tried in summary court-martial. It was revealed that they were disciplined, but not the manner of their punishment. But the trials of these men were not yet over; some of them would be called by Coakley as prosecution witnesses to testify against the fifty defendants.

On the first day of the trial each of the accused men was called before the court and asked how he pleaded to the charges. All of them pleaded not guilty.

The prosecution then began its presentation. Judge Advocate Coakley first called several officers to recount the events of the work stoppage and its aftermath. One of them was Commander Joseph R. Tobin, who was commanding officer of the Ryder Street Naval Barracks. Tobin testified that with the arrival of the U.S.S. *San Gay* on Tuesday, August 8, he ordered that the Fourth Port Chicago Division be alerted and ready to begin loading of the *San Gay* with ammunition the following day. Shortly after noon the next day Tobin said he was informed by Lieutenant Commander C. L. Bridges, executive officer, that the Fourth Division refused to work. Tobin then told Lieutenant Ernest Delucchi, the division officer, to order the men to work. Subsequently, he had the men brought before him individually. He spoke with six or seven of the men, he said, and ordered them to work. The men responded that they were afraid to handle ammunition. A phone call interrupted Tobin with the disturbing news that the Second and Eighth Divisions had also refused to work. Tobin instructed Lieutenant James E. Tobin (no relation), Second Division officer, and Lieutenant Carleton Morehouse, Eighth Division leader, to get their men back in formation and order them to work. Commander Tobin himself did not further talk with the enlisted men. Some 258 men still refused to work, Tobin testified, and they were then placed on a barge.

In cross-examination the defense established that although fifty men were on trial for refusing to work, Commander Tobin could not say from personal knowledge that any of them, with the exception of the six or seven he interviewed, were ever ordered to work. He also admitted that the men he spoke with said they were willing to obey all orders except an order to load ammunition. Under Veltmann's probing questioning, Tobin further admitted that the men were not riotous or disrepectful in their behavior.

Prosecutor Coakley then called to the stand a key witness, Lieutenant Ernest Delucchi, commanding officer of the recalcitrant Fourth Division. Delucchi, a thirty-four-year-old schoolteacher from San Francisco, had enlisted in 1941 and taken officers' training at Annapolis. He arrived at Port Chicago in October 1943 and was put in charge of Division Four.

Delucchi looked across the courtroom and identified twenty-five of the accused men as members of his division. He told of the division being quartered at Camp Shoemaker immediately after the Port Chicago explosion, and of their transfer to Mare Island Ammunition Depot on July 31. Upon learning on August 8 that his division was being assigned to load the *San Gay*, Delucchi said he told his division leader, Coxswain Elmer Boyer, "to notify all of the men in the division that they were going to have to load ammunition on the ninth of August." (Boyer was later called by the defense and testified that Delucchi did not say anything to him about loading ammunition before the muster on August 9.) The next day, Delucchi said, he went over to the barracks shortly before 11:30 A.M. to muster the division. He noticed that members of the Eighth Division were also standing around near the barracks. He claimed that he heard some of these men say, "Don't go to work for the white motherfuckers." Delucchi couldn't identify who said this because he was standing with his back to the Eighth Division men, facing his own division. Veltmann rose to object to Delucchi's statement. Coakley responded that this was evidence of a conspiracy. The objection was overruled.

After mustering, Delucchi ordered the 105 men of his division to march. When they came to the "T" in the road, he gave the fateful "Column left" order. "At that time one man by the name of Richmond began to lag back and look over his shoulder, in other words pushing back into the bunch following behind. . . . I immediately told this man . . . if he wasn't going to obey orders to fall out, and with that, why, practically the whole division fell out." Flabbergasted, Delucchi ordered his petty officer "to get the names of the men that were willing to go to work." Then he shoved off to report the incident to his commanding officer. Delucchi talked with Commander Tobin, he said, who told him to have the men stand fast. He then returned to where his division was standing to await the arrival of Commander Tobin. Meanwhile, Chaplain Flowers showed up and talked to the men while Delucchi contacted the naval barracks and requested that a shore patrol detail stand by.

After Chaplain Flowers finished, Delucchi said he marched his men to the parade ground, where he addressed them from the reviewing stand. "I told them that first of all we had never had any trouble like this at the base, certainly that they were letting the colored people down if they refused to work, and I told them that they took an oath like I did to obey orders while they were in the service. I told them that there were a lot of people who were working for the Negro people who also had sons and daughters and relatives on the other side that were fighting and that it wouldn't help the Negro people any if those people withdrew their support when they found out about how these men were acting. I pointed out to them that some of them were over on Mare Island when a destroyer came in that was torpedoed amidships, and I also pointed out that they didn't see the men of the destroyer going over the side and quitting the ship. . . ."

Delucchi was interrupted by defense attorney Veltmann, who objected that Delucchi's opinions were immaterial to the charge in the case. Veltmann also observed that Delucchi's testimony did not indicate that a direct order to work was given to the men. Veltmann's objection was overruled by the court.

Delucchi continued that by this time Commander Tobin had showed up and had him move the men over to the recreation building, where they were to be questioned one by one in alphabetical order. Delucchi sat in on the interrogation of the men that followed.

Afterward Delucchi talked to some of the men and ordered them to go to work. He said he ordered seventeen men to work but only one of these, Edward Saunders, was now among the accused, although Delucchi said others also refused at that time. Meanwhile, Delucchi's petty officer had been collecting the names of men who were willing to work. By the end of the afternoon only 32 men out of the 105 in Division Four had agreed to work, Delucchi testified. Seventy-three still refused. Delucchi added that three other men, who were not present at the initial muster—Harry Grimes, Julius Dixson, and George Diamond—were subsequently ordered by him to work and refused. Grimes had previously been assigned as a mess cook. In any event, by the conclusion of the first day of testimony it appeared that Lieutenant Delucchi had given direct orders to work to only four of the twenty-five men in his division accused of mutiny.

On Friday, September 15, court opened with a long debate between prosecution and defense about the conspiracy charge. Coakley, attempting to lay a basis for his line of questioning, argued that in a conspiracy trial allegations by any member of the conspiracy were admissible against all members of the conspiracy. Veltmann objected that "a statement that applies to a particular accused cannot possibly apply to all of the accused." Further, Veltmann contended, Lieutenant Delucchi's testimony should apply only to the men he directly ordered to load ammunition; Delucchi's other comments should be stricken from the record. The court refused to strike Delucchi's testimony.

With that Delucchi was put back on the stand for the second day. He recounted the assembly of the men on the baseball diamond on August 11 to be addressed by Admiral Wright. After the admiral spoke, Delucchi approached his division and said he heard someone say, "The motherfuckers won't do anything to us; they are scared of us; they won't even send us to sea." Another voice added: "Let's run over the motherfuckers." Veltmann jumped up to object that this was hearsay from unidentified speakers. Again the court overruled the objection.

Delucchi then ordered his men to fall out into two groups— those willing to obey and those not willing to obey orders to handle ammunition. All but four men—Joe Small, Bennon Dees, Cecil Miller, and Ernest Brown—joined the willing group. Delucchi told his junior officer, Lieutenant Kaufmann, to take the names of the refusers, and then he left to speak with Commander Tobin and Captain Kinne. As he looked back he saw men moving from the willing to the unwilling side, "so that by the time I got back there I had twenty-two men lined up with Lieutenant Kaufmann taking their names signifying their willingness to disobey my orders." The refusers were then sent back to the barge. The next morning, according to Delucchi, three men who had initially been in the willing-to-work group now refused his orders to do so, thus bringing the number of refusers in Division Four to twenty-five.

Under cross-examination Delucchi admitted that some of the

men told him they were afraid of ammunition but that they would perform any other work and obey all other orders. Delucchi also admitted that among the men ordered to work that day and the next was one man, Ollie Green, who had his arm in a sling due to an accident. (Coakley objected that there were plenty of things a one-armed man could do on the ammunition dock.)

At the conclusion of his testimony Delucchi was routinely asked by the court whether he had anything else to say. Without further prompting Delucchi revealed that two of the men he had ordered to work he did not consider "up to par." One of these men, Julius Dixson, had a nervous condition and, Delucchi offered, was previously excluded from handling ammunition, being considered a liability on the loading pier, and instead permanently assigned by Delucchi as a mess cook.

Why he would order men he did not consider "up to par" to load ammunition was not asked of Delucchi, and with his curious remark the second day of the trial ended.

When Commander Tobin was called away by news of the revolt by the Second and Eighth Divisions, his executive officer, Charles Bridges, took over the interrogation of the Fourth Division. Bridges, called as the first witness when court reconvened at 10:00 A.M. Saturday, September 16, said that he interviewed thirty-one men and ordered them to work. Of these thirty-one men, twenty-five refused to go to work, of whom seven were now among the defendants. (He was unable to identify any of them when asked to do so.) Questioned by Lieutenant Veltmann, Bridges said that the men told him they were afraid of handling ammunition. Bridges, who was at the assembly at which Admiral Wright spoke, and standing only ten or fifteen feet from the Fourth Division, said he heard no epithets uttered by the men.

Chaplain Flowers recalled his encounter with the men and his offer to go into the hold with them. Flowers described the men as very respectful, but not persuaded by his efforts. When he referred to the soldiers in foxholes on the front lines, the refusers responded that "you can fight back in that case, but you can't fight back in this case if anything happens and it blows up."

Flowers was assigned to talk with twenty-eight of the Fourth Division men individually about whether they would load ammunition. Twenty of these refused, he said. "Did the men say, 'I refuse to handle ammunition?' Veltmann inquired. "No, sir; they said, 'I am afraid to handle ammunition; I will obey any other orders, but I will not go over and handle ammunition.' " Flowers added that some of the men appeared to be frightened and others evidenced similar strain. Every one of the twenty-eight men said he was afraid, the chaplain recounted. Some asked him about survivors' leaves.

Meanwhile, orders had gone out for the Second and Eighth Divisions to be mustered for work. Lieutenant Carleton Morehouse, division officer of the Eighth Division, testified that he attempted to muster his men about 1:30 in the afternoon of August 9 in front of the barracks. Morehouse addressed the men and told them they were being assigned to load ammunition. He ordered any who refused to work to fall out. Pandemonium broke out as some of the men began shouting and milling about. Morehouse reported the matter to Commander Tobin, who told him to order the men individually to work. Morehouse mustered the men again and called off the names alphabetically and ordered each man to work. Ninety-six of the 104 men in the division refused. They were ordered to the barge with the Fourth Division refusers. Two days later, after hearing Admiral Wright's warnings, all of the reluctant Eighth Division men agreed to go back to work. Consequently, there were no members of the Eighth Division on trial. The relevance of Morehouse's testimony might have been questioned by the defense, but was not. Instead, Veltmann deftly elicited that some of Morehouse's men had told him they were afraid to handle ammunition before the work stoppage. Coakley quickly objected to this line of questioning as hearsay, and was sustained.

As for the Second Division, some of its members had remained at Port Chicago after the explosion to help with the cleanup operation; others were transferred to Camp Shoemaker. By the end of July all of the men were back at Port Chicago.

On August 8, according to Lieutenant James Tobin, these men were mustered at the rebuilt barracks in Port Chicago. Lieutenant Tobin told them they were to load ammunition aboard the U.S.S. *San Gay* at Mare Island the next day. "I said to them that I knew of some who were scared but that there was no reason to be particularly scared of loading ammunition at Mare Island, that we would not load such hazardous type of ammunition as we had loaded at Port Chicago; that there had to be an element of trust on the part of all hands; that I had faith in them and they would have to have faith in me as I would be present with them, and I reminded them how carefully we had handled ammunition that very afternoon which was of a very sensitive nature, and I told them that we shouldn't experience any difficulty over here because most of the ammunition would be gun ammunition."

The next day, August 9, the men of the division were loaded onto five buses for the ride down to Mare Island, arriving in Vallejo a little after 2:00 in the afternoon. Lieutenant Tobin, who had come down separately and gotten word of the work refusals, assembled his men; his first words to them were: "Many men from the other divisions have refused to obey orders." This was not meant to be a prompt, but if any of the men in the Second Division did not know what had happened, they certainly did now. Tobin warned the men that refusal to obey orders in wartime carried serious consequences. He then said that any men who refused to obey orders to load ammunition should step to one side. A large group of men moved to one side, he reported. He then spoke with Commander Tobin and returned to order his men individually to work. Eighty-seven of the men still refused and were ordered to the barge. After the admiral spoke on the 11th the men were mustered again, and this time the number of refusers was reduced to twenty-two. The next day, Lieutenant Tobin continued, three men who had originally indicated they would return to work did not do so. Tobin confronted the three, who told him they were afraid. They refused to work, he said, and he ordered them confined. Tobin later admitted that one of the defendants from his division, John Dunn, had never been assigned to load ammunition before because he was underweight, weighing only 104 pounds.

Most of the remainder of the prosecution case over the next days was made up of testimony by enlisted men—not the defendants —from the Second, Fourth, and Eighth Divisions. Some of these men, Veltmann drew out, were already convicted in summary court-martials for their involvement in the work refusal. Their sentences were not revealed. (Some of these witnesses were still confined to the stockade at the time they were called to testify.) In general these men testified that in the days leading up to August 9, there had been talk—rather vague and ambiguous talk, Veltmann countered—about not going back to work and that a "don't work" list was circulated. Some said that Joe Small spoke at the barge meeting and urged the men to stick together, and to obey the shore patrol and the officers. (One man said Small added that the men had the officers "by the ass"; another man said Small referred to having the officers "by the tail.") That Small urged the men to be orderly and not give trouble to the guards or officers was stressed in cross-examination by the defense. When some of these witnesses became evasive under the prosecutor's probing, Coakley referred to the written statements they had made earlier during interrogation. Veltmannn objected to introducing the statements as evidence, but in a critical ruling the court allowed Coakley to use the statements to refresh the men's memories, meaning he could present the statements to them and then have them verify or deny what was written. One of the witnesses, Edward Stubblefield, an enlisted seaman in the Eighth Division, claimed that Joe Small threatened the men, saying, "If any of the guys back out we would beat them up or something." Another witness, Eighth Division man Clarence Morgan, reported under cross-examination that some of the men did indeed try to give up the resistance and go back to work, but it was the officers who wouldn't let them leave the barge.

A Fourth Division man, Joseph Gray, testified that at the Ryder Street barracks he was given a sheet of paper by another enlisted man. At the top of the paper were the words "We, the undersigned men, are willing to work, but refuse to load ammunition." Gray said he signed the paper and noted that about sixty other men had also signed it. When questioned by Veltmann, Gray admitted that the language on the paper may have said the undersigned men "don't want to handle ammunition" rather than "refuse" to handle ammunition. Gray admitted that he had pleaded guilty to disobeying orders in a summary court-martial—and now he was testifying in a trial in which one of the defendants was his own brother, Charles Gray, also a Fourth Division man.

Lieutenant Commander Coakley wrapped up the prosecution case on Friday, September 22. The testimony he had presented was aimed to show that there had been a conspiracy among the enlisted men from Port Chicago to refuse to obey orders to load ammunition. This constituted mutiny, according to Coakley. But the objections and counterarguments by the defense made it clear that the defense did not accept the mutiny charge as presented, nor did the defense agree that there was a conspiracy among the men. Moreover, the defense contended that if direct orders to load ammunition were given, they were not given to all of the men. Hence, they could not all be guilty, even of only refusing to obey orders. Another sore point between the defense and prosecution was whether and how Coakley could use the written statements taken from the men during interrogation. On all of these points the court had basically sided with Coakley's viewpoint, sometimes after initial waffling. The defense may have raised some doubts about whether all the men, especially those in the Fourth Division, were directly ordered to work. But this small plus was largely overshadowed by Coakley's orchestration of a torrent of testimony about the alleged conspiracy. Even if most of that testimony was only hearsay and ambiguous, and only a few of the defendants were identified by name, the impression was left of agitators and ring-leaders browbeating the others into mutinous rebellion.

Lieutenant Veltmann and his five assistants retired to the little office provided for them in the administration building and re-viewed one more time their plan for the defense.

CHAPTER

8

The Mutiny Trial: Defense

The defense opened with what appeared to be an important victory. The court ruled in favor of defense attorney Veltmann's motion that the testimony of Commander Joseph Tobin, Lieutenant Ernest Delucchi, and the other division officers would apply only to the defendants they identified by name as having been given direct orders to work. A favorable ruling in principle but meaningless in practice if the court did not keep careful track of the individual names mentioned by officers and the nature of the reference. (Bouts of drowsiness afflicted everyone in the courtroom, but one member of Osterhaus's court was notorious among the reporters for regularly nodding off during the proceedings.)

The defense plan was to call all of the defendants one by one to testify on their own behalf. The tone of the testimony by most of the defendants was set by the first man to be called, Seaman Edward L. Longmire, of the Second Port Chicago Division. Longmire, an eighteen-year-old former poultry salesman from Cincinnati, Ohio, briefly recalled the night of the explosion; he was not injured and he helped another youth who had broken glass embedded in his arm. The next day, he continued, he was with that part of his division taken to Camp Stoneman and then transferred to Camp

Shoemaker. Arriving back at Port Chicago at the end of July the men worked on dunnage piles for a week.

This brought Longmire to August 9 in his testimony. On the bus ride from Port Chicago to Mare Island he said the men talked of their fear of ammunition and the possibility of another explosion. Being en route they did not know of the trouble happening at that moment in Vallejo. When the buses pulled up to the naval barracks in Vallejo, Longmire noticed a lot of shore patrolmen, guards, standing nearby. The men got off the buses and mustered. The division officer, Lieutenant Tobin, showed up and spoke. He urged them not to be fearful and to trust him. Then he ordered them to fall out into groups willing or unwilling to obey all orders. Confusion followed. Tobin left for a moment, Longmire said. When Tobin returned he had the men line up again in their regular working formation. This meant that Longmire, who was the smallest in the group, was now standing last in line, all the way to one side.

The men were then ordered to peel off one at a time, which made Longmire first. He said Lieutenant Tobin spoke with him and asked Longmire if he was willing to obey all lawful orders. Longmire responded, "Yes, sir, but I am afraid of ammunition." Tobin then told him to give his name to Tobin's assistant, Lieutenant Clement, who was writing down the names of the work refusers. Some prosecution witnesses had said there was cheering and backslapping after the men gave their names to Lieutenant Clement; Longmire said this was not true. The work refusers were then marched to the barge.

On the barge Longmire attended the meeting at which Joe Small spoke. He heard Small tell the men "to watch their conduct and cooperate with them shore patrol and officers and don't get in any more trouble." He didn't hear Small say anything about "having the officers by the balls." The meeting was over in a few minutes.

Longmire denied that anyone tried to persuade him to disobey orders, and said neither did he try to get men not to work.

After hearing the admiral's threat of having the men shot, Longmire went on, Lieutenant Tobin ordered all the men willing to obey orders to fall in line in front of him. "He [Tobin] was standing in front of the line with a little black notebook in his hand, and I got in line and I told him I was willing to obey orders but I was afraid to load ammunition. . . . He told me he ain't got time for no personal favors, that if anything was wrong with me they would take care of me, and he told me to get over by the fence, that he would talk to me later on, and then I got out of line and waited. After he took all of the men's names and got them lined up he walked back toward me and I left the fence to come out to meet him and he said, 'Get back in line.' I was hesitating and he said, 'It's too late . . . get in line with the other men,' and he took my name and brought us [to the barge]."

The men picked up their seabags at the barge and were then taken to the stockade at Camp Shoemaker. Longmire remembered being questioned by a lieutenant at Shoemaker. "He asked me what my name was and I told him. He asked me what year I had gone to in school and he asked me my age, and then he asked me about the meeting that Small gave. . . . He said, 'If you want us to help you you have got to help us.' I told him I was telling the truth, I didn't know none of the things he was talking about—having the officers by the balls—that is what I told him. He asked me did I tell anybody not to go to work and I told him, 'No, sir.' "

Later the lieutenant read the statement back to Longmire. Longmire disputed some of what was written, and the two got into a shouting match. But the statement was not changed, Longmire said. "He would never tell [the stenographer] to write the same thing as I said it was."

Longmire admitted that he signed the statement.

"Did anybody tell you you had to make a statement?" the defense attorney asked.

"No, sir, no one told me I had to make a statement, but they put it to you so funny—I couldn't say how they put it to you, I was afraid—anyway after they was talking about shooting I was afraid myself."

In cross-examination prosecutor Coakley tried to have Longmire's written statement introduced as evidence. Veltmann objected on grounds that the statement was "made under duress while the witness was a prisoner under guard, and is not a voluntary statement of the witness." Coakley countered that there was no evidence that the statement was taken under duress: "the mere fact that a statement might be taken after a man is arrested isn't any proof of duress." Veltmann and Coakley wrangled back and forth on the issue. Coakley suggested that the statements were not confessions, where the voluntary nature of the statement must be established, but merely "admissions" and consequently "no foundation of the free and voluntary character need be laid." The court ruled that the statement could not be introduced as evidence, but Coakley was to be allowed to ask questions of the defendant based on the statement.

Coakley then turned to Longmire.

"This statement, dated August 23, 1944, which you have read, and which you signed, [contains] the following statement: 'I temporarily slept on the top deck of the barge at Mare Island. . . . The reason I slept there was that the lieutenant [Tobin] asked the Second Division to handle ammunition and if any would not, to fall out and go aboard the barge.' That statement is in there?"

"Yes, sir."

"You didn't tell Lieutenant DuBois [the interrogating officer at Camp Shoemaker] on the 23rd of August when you talked to him, that Lieutenant Tobin said, 'Are you willing to obey all orders?' and that you said, 'Yes, but I am afraid of ammunition'?"

"He didn't ask me that, sir."

Under further questioning by Coakley, Longmire repeated his earlier testimony that before August 9 some men talked about being afraid of another accident and said they were fearful of handling ammunition, but he heard no one say they were in fact not going to obey orders to load ammunition.

The court recessed at noon for lunch. That afternoon Coakley continued to drill Longmire, but the young man would not budge from the testimony he had given that morning, denying that he had ever received a direct order to load ammunition. It was a grueling session, but Longmire held firm and refused to be cowed by Coakley. As the lead-off defendant, Longmire showed that the accused men had a case of their own to make.

Following Longmire on the stand was Seaman Ollie E. Green, an enlisted man in the Fourth Division. A truck driver from Washington, D.C., at thirty-seven years of age Green was one of the oldest men in the group. Green said he was injured by flying glass in the explosion and hospitalized. Upon release he was sent to Vallejo, where his unit was now stationed. On August 8 Green fractured his wrist in an accident and was placed on the sick list. He was not with the division when it mustered the next day, but he was in the barracks and shortly afterward he came downstairs and saw the men in disarray in front of Lieutenant Delucchi. "Some of the boys were standing up, some sitting on the grass. Lieutenant

Delucchi was standing up there talking to the petty officer." Delucchi reassembled the men at a reviewing stand and spoke to them, Green recalled. Standing in the back with his arm in a sling, he could barely make out what was being said, something about "letting him down." He said he never heard an order to work issued. Green was one of the men questioned by Chaplain Flowers.

"He asked me was I going to work, and I told him, 'No, sir.'"

"What else did he say?"

"Well, he spoke to me first about my hand. He asked me how was my hand getting along and I said, 'Not so good.'"

"What did he say to you about going to work?"

"That is all he asked me about going to work; he never gave me no order, sir."

Confined to the barge with other refusers, Green missed Joe Small's meeting because he was playing cards (and he later admitted that he actually made his living in civilian life through "games of chance"), but he was there when the admiral spoke. Describing Lieutenant Delucchi's separation of the willing from the unwilling men, Green sometimes gave the impression of confusing his lines: "Lieutenant Delucchi gave us an order, I mean, didn't give us an order, asked us, 'All who are willing to obey any kind of order step off over on the west side and the ones who didn't want to, step over on the east side.' So, the majority of the division stepped over on the west side and then some of them started mixing back over on the east side." Green ended up on the east side.

When cross-examined by Coakley, Green said that if he had been ordered to load ammunition before he broke his wrist on August 8 he would have done so, but he added that he was also afraid of ammunition after the explosion. He denied, however, that he was ever given a direct order to load ammunition at any time during the work stoppage.

"The chaplain asked me was I willing to go to work and I told him, 'No, sir.'"

"You heard him testify that he gave you an order," Coakley shot back. "Didn't he?"

"I know, but he didn't give me no order."

Stalemated, Coakley decided to call it quits. Admiral Osterhaus routinely asked Green if he had anything further to say.

"I got a couple of things to say, sir," Green responded, surprising everyone. "The reason I was afraid to go down and load ammunition, them officers [were] racing each division to see who put on the most tonnage, and I knowed the way they was handling ammunition, it was liable to go off again."

Green paused. The courtroom waited in stunned silence.

"If we didn't work fast at that time, they wanted to put us in the brig, and when the exec [executive officer] came down on the docks, they wanted us to slow up. That is exactly the way—put it on fast; if we didn't put it on fast they want to put us in the brig. That is my reason for not going down there."

If there was a defense script, this was not part of it. Veltmann was as surprised as Coakley; the defense had no intention of raising questions about working conditions at Port Chicago. But it happened so quickly; Green finished and was off the stand before a single objection could be raised.

The newspaper reporters picked up Green's statement about racing and featured it in the papers the next day. Naval authorities quickly issued a statement denying Green's charge.

After Green's startling disclosure the remainder of the day was anticlimactic, but not without interest. John H. Dunn, the slender seventeen-year-old Second Division mess cook from Brooklyn, testified that he had never before handled ammunition because a doctor had said that at 104 pounds he was "too light to work on the dock." Coakley asked if Lieutenant Tobin had not given him orders, but Dunn denied being directly ordered to load ammunition.

Wednesday, September 27, was the twelfth day of the great mutiny trial. The Allies were advancing steadily on the western front in Europe, and in the Pacific a U.S. carrier fleet was shelling Luzon in the Philippines in preparation for a landing. On Treasure Island the struggle in the courtroom became more intense as the defense called Seaman First Class Joseph R. Small to the stand to testify. Sitting alertly in his dress blues, Small gave his name and rank and said that his present station was the general court-martial brig. As the alleged "ringleader" of the mutiny, Small could make or break the defense; and prosecutor Coakley would be listening carefully as he prepared his questions for the cross-examination.

Small said he came to Port Chicago on October 3, 1943, and within a few days he was under Lieutenant Delucchi's command in the Fourth Division. He said that he was in the barracks the night of the explosion. "During the explosion I was thrown out of my bed and got a few cuts around," he said. "All the men were running wild here and there, and I started for the back door but the porch fell before I got there, so I stopped. Then I got myself together and turned to help the other men out, the men that were injured."

After the transfer next day to Camp Shoemaker, he continued, the men were jittery, and talking of the fear of ammunition. He recounted the incident of the men's panic in the Shoemaker barracks when a piece of paper "got some way hooked in the fan and made a queer noise." After another similar incident the men were upset with the man who caused the commotion. "I quieted them down and got them back to bed," Small said.

There were no meetings held by the enlisted men at Camp Shoemaker, Small testified, and no one tried to convince him not to load ammunition; neither did he try to persuade others.

Small continued that on the morning of August 9 he was told by petty officer Elmer Boyer that the men were to fall out for a muster. At the time Small and eleven other Fourth Division men were bunking on the lower floor of the two-story barracks building, with the Second Division men. The rest of the Fourth Division was on the upper deck. Small helped to muster the Fourth Division in front of the barracks. The men were then ordered to move out.

When Delucchi gave the "Column left" order, the men stopped, Small said. Delucchi spoke to the man called Richmond, and "practically all the rest of [the men] fell out." (Richmond was not one of the defendants, and oddly he was never called by the prosecution or the defense to testify as a witness.)

"What happened then?"

"Well, nothing happened for the next few moments; they all stood up and looked. Then the next thing I noticed Boyer was writing names on a piece of paper."

"Continue."

"Lieutenant Delucchi was standing up there. He was talking with the other lieutenant and some commander of the division, and I walked off to Boyer to find out what the names were for, but I never got a chance; Lieutenant Delucchi spoke to me."

"What did he say to you?"

"He asked me was my name on the list. I told him, 'No, sir.' "

"Did he ask you why?"

"Yes, sir, he asked me why. I told him that if the list pertained to men loading ammunition, I didn't intend for my name to be on it."

"Why not?"

"I was afraid of ammunition. I told him I would obey any order except the order to load ammunition."

Small said he was later interviewed by Chaplain Flowers.

"He explained to me the position I was in. He told me that I was doing wrong and he asked me if I would consider loading ammunition."

"What did you answer to that?"

" 'No, sir.' "

"Then what happened?"

"He said, 'Ball field, next man.' I was taken out by the seaman guard and sent over to the ball field."

Neither Lieutenant Delucchi nor Chaplain Flowers ever gave him a direct order to load ammunition, Small stated.

Small also denied seeing or signing a list of names of men who refused to load ammunition.

After the men were interviewed at the recreation building on August 9, Small continued, Lieutenant Delucchi had him assemble the men who were being sent to the barge. "We marched from there to the barracks. [Lieutenant Delucchi] told me to see that they got their gear and went down to the barge. I did. He told me that we were to be quartered topside, inboard and there was to be no smoking, and I was to see to it that no rough stuff was carried on. . . . He told me, 'I am putting you in charge . . . and I am giving you three men to work under you, and out of you four, you ought to be able to keep things straight.' "

On the barge the evening of August 10, after the fight in the chow hall, Small met with the other acting petty officers assigned to keep order. They talked over the situation. They called in one of the men who had been making trouble, and Small warned him about his behavior. Then, though it was late, they decided to call a meeting of all the men on the lower deck of the barge.

About fifteen minutes before taps the men assembled on the lower deck, Small continued, and then he stepped forward to speak.

"I stepped out where I thought that everyone could see me. I said, 'All right, fellows, knock it off, listen to what is to be said. It is as much for your good as it is for mine.' Then I went on to tell them that they had to knock off the horseplay, obey the shore patrol, take orders that were given to them by the officers, or else it might result in them calling in the marines. I told them it would be much worse under marine guard than it was at the present time; that they could make it much better for themselves if they would cooperate in that respect. I told them also if they pulled together, they would find out that things would be much easier for them."

"What did you mean by that, Small?"

"I meant to pull together in keeping themselves straight, one to the other; if one got off wrong, it was up to his shipmate, his pal, whoever it might be, to tell him to 'Straighten up and fly right,' knock it off, get back in line."

"In other words," defense attorney Veltmann suggested, "you meant to keep order, isn't that what you meant?"

"Yes, sir."

"Did you make the statement attributed to you by other witnesses that 'We have the officers by the ass'?"

"No, sir."

"Or 'We have the officers by the tail'?"

"No, sir."

"Or 'We have the officers by the balls'?"

"No, sir."

"Did you make the statement 'If we stick together, they can't do anything to us'?"

"No, sir."

"How long did the meeting last, Small?"

"Approximately four minutes."

"What happened after you finished talking?"

"Well, there was applauding, hand shaking—I mean, clapping, and a few of the fellows said, 'That's good,' with a few swears in it, such as 'That's damn good, maybe we'll get something out of it,' and I returned to the topside."

Small's denial of having said things at the meeting which he did in fact say was probably dismissed by the court; that he admitted speaking at all was damning enough.

The next day after the admiral's talk, Small continued, Lieutenant Delucchi ordered his men to fall out into groups willing or unwilling to obey all orders. At first confused by Delucchi's wording, Small joined the willing group. "At that time I realized that the order could be to load ammunition and that's one order I was—that I wasn't willing to obey."

"Why not?"

"I was afraid of ammunition."

The refusers were transferred to the brig at Camp Shoemaker and Small placed in solitary confinement. Small said he was later questioned by a lieutenant at Shoemaker. "I didn't know at that time that I was making a statement. The lieutenant merely asked me a lot of questions and I answered them to the best way I could and he later brought them to me to sign."

"Did you sign them?"

"I did sign them, yes, sir."

"Why did you sign them?"

"Well, he told me to sign them, I was under orders from him, he just shoved them and said, 'Sign them,' and so I signed them."

With that Lieutenant Veltmann ended his direct examination of Joe Small; now prosecutor Coakley would have his turn.

Coakley began by eliciting that Small was twenty-three years old and had lived in New Jersey and was a truck driver before he came in the service. Small spoke with a decidedly northern accent.

Confronting Small about his interview and statements at Camp Shoemaker, Coakley bore down.

"Now, in that conversation you were asked about a meeting on the barge, weren't you?"

"Yes, sir."

"You were asked who suggested that the meeting be called, weren't you?"

"Yes, sir."

"You said in answer to the question, 'All the petty officers [referring to the four men assigned to keep order], one is as much to blame as the other, I guess,' didn't you?"

"I can't readily remember whether that was the answer or not."

"You didn't say that?"

"No, sir."

"With reference to that same conversation I will ask you whether or not this question was asked of you and the answer given: 'Q. What occurred at the meeting? A. I just warned them against rioting with the shore patrol, fighting, smoking when they weren't supposed to, disobedience of orders—not getting in line and marching right. I just asked them to cooperate with the shore patrol, because they were more for us than they were against us.'"

"Yes, sir."

(The seaman guard and shore patrol members were all black; the marine guards were white.)

"Now then, you called the meeting, didn't you?"

"Well, that's where all the petty officers come in—one is as much to blame as the other."

"In that conversation I will ask you whether or not these questions were asked of you and these answers given: 'Q. Who called the meeting? A. I did, sir. Q. How was the meeting called? A. I just went through the barge and asked all the men to gather on the lower deck.' Were those questions asked you and those answers given?"

"Well, they were asked, but it wasn't exactly that way, that is not exactly the answer."

"I will ask you again, when you were asked the question who called the meeting, did you say, 'I did, sir'?"

"I did, I had a part in calling it."

Unable to get Small to perjure himself, Coakley asked whether Small knew before August 9 that the men would be assigned to loading ammunition. Small said that petty officer Boyer mentioned that the men would be loading a ship on Thursday, August 10, but they did not know what work they would be doing on August 9 before the "Column left" order. Small admitted that before that, he had made up his mind that he was not going to handle ammunition.

It was almost noon, so Osterhaus ordered that the court recess until 1:15 for lunch. It had been a long morning, and Small's questioning was not over yet.

After lunch, Small was back on the witness stand. Prodded by Coakley, Small admitted that "practically everybody in the division" talked about whether they would return to loading ships in the days before the work stoppage, but he refused to give the names of men who talked, saying it was the whole division.

As the afternoon wore on they again went over the events of the work stoppage and after, and Small's testimony remained essentially the same. He continued to deny that he was ever ordered to load ammunition. Unable to shake Small from his testimony, Coakley let him leave the stand.

In the following days more of the defendants took the stand to testify. In general they said they were willing to obey orders, but they were afraid to handle ammunition, especially since the July

17 explosion in which some of them had been injured and later hospitalized. Most of them contended that they were not given direct orders to load ammunition, but rather were asked whether or not they were willing to obey orders that might be given; because of their fear, they failed to join, or remain in, the willing group. They asserted that they did not try to influence anyone not to work, nor were they so influenced by others. As for signing a list of the men afraid to handle ammunition—some said they had, others never saw or signed a list. Some were at the barge meeting; others not. Those who attended testified that Small said to stop making trouble, obey the guards and officers, and stick together. Under cross-examination many of them denied the accuracy of the written statements taken while they were imprisoned at Camp Shoemaker before the trial.

Jack Crittenden, seaman Second Division, testified that his division officer, Lieutenant Tobin, never ordered him to load ammunition, and that he was willing to do so and stood in the willing group after hearing the admiral speak. But the next day, when he was late joining the division for work duty, Lieutenant Tobin had him sent to the brig, Crittenden said. That was how his name was added to the ranks of the accused. Charles Gray, whose brother, Joseph Gray, had earlier been called by the prosecution to testify, admitted that he was one of those who signed the list of those who didn't want to handle ammunition. He did not say how or why he and his brother, who was also in the Fourth Division but agreed to work, parted ways. Ernest D. Brown, another Fourth Division man, was one of the few who refused to sign a statement at Camp Shoemaker. He stood on his constitutional rights, he testified, not to make a statement.

With the trial now into its third week in early October, nineteen-year-old Julius Dixson, one of the seamen whom Lieutenant Delucchi described as not up to par, said that he suffered dizzy spells and that a doctor had taken him off dock work; for the three months prior to the Port Chicago explosion he had been a mess cook. Lieutenant Veltmann also pointed out that the statement supposedly made by Dixson at Shoemaker was in fact written in the third person.

The pattern of the defense was now clear and it seemed there would be no surprises. The testimony was settling into a routine: the men were afraid, they did not conspire, there were no direct orders issued. But on Wednesday, October 4, the eighteenth day of the trial, the court was brought bolt upright when defendant Alphonso McPherson, a Second Division man, charged that prosecutor Coakley threatened to have him shot. McPherson testified that while he was imprisoned at Camp Shoemaker after the work stoppage he was interrogated by Coakley. When he balked at responding to some of the questions, he said, Coakley told him, "I am going to give you another chance, but if you don't come clean this time I am going to see that you get shot." When confronted on the stand by Coakley himself, McPherson stuck to his charge.

McPherson added that he had suffered internal injuries in the explosion and that he was still in pain and that was why he did not load ammunition. Coakley responded by suggesting that McPherson was a chronic complainer. (Two days later the trial was interrupted by news that McPherson had been rushed to the hospital seriously ill with a double hernia.)

Coakley and Veltmann got into a heated wrangle over the shooting charge, with Coakley denying that he threatened anyone and saying this was a personal affront and Veltmann denying that he knew McPherson was going to make the accusation. (The next day Coakley also issued a statement to the press denying the charge, and suggesting that Veltmann had coached the witness.) The brawl between the two attorneys continued until Admiral Osterhaus observed that McPherson had not been shot and it was time to break for lunch.

On October 9, two months after the work stoppage and the twenty-second day of the mutiny trial, matters took another unusual turn. Sitting in on the proceedings that Monday was Thurgood Marshall, chief counsel for the NAACP. Marshall had just arrived by plane from New York, with special travel priority arranged by Secretary of the Navy Forrestal. Earlier, Joseph James, president of the San Francisco branch of the NAACP, had telephoned the national office in New York alerting them to the importance of the case. Marshall's visit was in response to James's call, and also because, as he explained later, of the "great feeling in the East over the Navy's policy of giving Negroes all the dirty and dangerous work."

Well acquainted with the legal struggle against racial discrimination, Thurgood Marshall was a lawyer with a mission. Born in

1908 in Baltimore, Marshall's intelligent and strongly antisegregationist parents encouraged him as a youth to get a good education, and they fostered his interest in civil rights. He graduated from Lincoln University in Pennsylvania in 1930 and received his law degree from Howard University in 1933, graduating first in his class. At Howard his teachers included Charles Houston, William Hastie, and James Nabrit, men who were in the forefront of civil rights law through their work with the NAACP. Returning to Baltimore and entering private practice, Marshall volunteered his services to the local branch of the NAACP. His first case involved a black student who was seeking admission to the University of North Carolina; the case was lost on a technicality. Later, in 1935, Marshall won his first case for the NAACP, compelling the University of Maryland Law School to admit a black student. In a statement that foretold his lifelong approach to law, Marshall argued, "What's at stake here is more than the rights of my clients; it's the moral commitment stated in our nation's creed."

In 1935 Charles Houston joined the national staff of the NAACP in New York as special counsel; a year later he invited his former student to become his assistant. Marshall accepted. By 1944 Marshall and the NAACP were no strangers to the problems of black men in the military. Two years younger than Marshall, the NAACP was founded in 1910 to challenge racially discriminatory laws and practices in American society. Its legal department often got involved in military cases where there appeared to be an element of discrimination in the treatment of black servicemen. In 1939 the legal department was spun off as the NAACP Legal Defense and Educational Fund, and Marshall was offered the post of director-counsel. Marshall argued his first case before the U.S. Supreme Court in 1942, defending three black soldiers accused of rape. (In his career he would go on to argue thirty-two cases before the Supreme Court, winning twenty-nine of them, including the famous *Brown* v. *Board of Education* case in 1954 that led to the desegregation of public schools.)

At the Treasure Island mutiny trial Marshall heard defendants Theodore King, Martin Bordenave, Charles David, Cyril Sheppard, and Mentor Burns testify on his first day at the trial. Their testimony was much like that of the other defendants; there was nothing unusual about it except that prosecutor Coakley in his cross-examination took special pains to establish which of the men were from the North. Marshall also met with the defendants and talked with their attorneys.

The next day, Tuesday, October 10, Marshall held a press conference with the news reporters covering the trial. The newspapers headlined his charge that prosecutor Coakley was prejudiced in his handling of the case. From his conversations with the men and review of the record, Marshall was reported as saying, he saw no reasons why the men should be tried for mutiny, which implies a mass conspiracy, rather than on lesser charges of individual insubordination. He suggested that Coakley's calling attention to the northern men was meant to imply that they were the leaders of a mutinous conspiracy.

"The men actually don't know what happened," he said. "Had they been given a direct and specific order to load ammunition and they had refused to obey that order then the charge would be legitimate. But they say no direct order to load was issued them. They were asked whether they would load and they replied that they were afraid. They have told me they were willing to go to jail to get a change of duty because of their terrific fear of explosives, but they had no idea that verbal expression of their fear constituted mutiny."

Although Marshall praised the Navy defense officers to the press as "doing an excellent job," he was already thinking about larger issues of the trial which were not being brought out at the proceedings.

Coakley did not publicly reply to Marshall's accusations, but his anger flashed in the courtroom that Tuesday. When defendant Frank Henry neglected to say "sir" in answer to one of Coakley's questions, the prosecutor snapped, "Did you learn to say 'sir' when you talk to an officer, did you learn that? . . . Why don't you say it instead of being so insolent?"

Marshall, who was not saying "sir" to anybody, followed the proceedings for the remainder of the week. The last of the defendants were called to the stand to testify and spoke of their fear. Their testimony was buttressed by Navy psychiatrist Richard H. Pembroke, who testified for the defense that indeed the experience of the huge explosion would generate fear, and that "fear is a condition which prepares the body organism for impending or anticipated action protective in nature."

Elmer Boyer, Lieutenant Delucchi's chief petty officer in the Fourth Division, called by the defense to testify, said that Delucchi told him nothing about loading ammunition before August 9. At the muster that day Boyer, who never refused to work and was not one of the defendants, said he heard no derogatory remarks by any of the men. He said it came as a "surprise to everybody" when the men broke ranks after the "Column left" order. Boyer then asked the men, "What men are going to work?" The majority of the men fell out, and he began writing names in his notebook. Boyer said that at no time did he ever hear Lieutenant Delucchi give any of the men a direct order to load ammunition.

With the defense presentation completed and the trial over for the week, Thurgood Marshall met with local NAACP officials over the weekend and attended a meeting of the San Francisco branch the following Monday, October 16. Marshall declared that "this is not an individual case. This is not fifty men on trial for mutiny. This is the Navy on trial for its whole vicious policy toward Negroes." Continuing, he said: "Negroes are not afraid of anything any more than anyone else. Negroes in the Navy don't mind loading ammunition. They just want to know why they are the only ones doing the loading! They wanted to know why they are segregated; why they don't get promoted."

Marshall was not alone in his concern about racial discrimination in the military. The week before, fifty pastors of black churches in the Bay Area had urged their congregations to sign a petition to President Roosevelt demanding that he, as Commander in Chief, "issue an executive order to stop discrimination against . . . Negroes in the armed services."

Sensing that the time was right to press the larger issues raised by the trial, Marshall the next day called for a formal investigation by the government of the circumstances leading to the work stoppage. He identified three aspects of the affair that required special attention:

> 1. The policy of the 12th Naval District which, with only a few minor exceptions, restricts the use of Negro seamen, regardless of their training and qualifications, to shore duty in the capacity of laborers and in segregated outfits.
>
> 2. The inefficient and unsafe manner in which ammunition was handled at Port Chicago prior to the explosion,

and the fact that Negroes working on it are given absolutely no kind of instruction or training in the proper handling of it.

3. The inconsistent, haphazard and utterly unfair manner in which the 50 accused seamen now on trial for their lives were singled out from [other] men, whose actions with regard to the loading of ammunition after the Port Chicago explosion, were identical in almost every respect to those of the 50 accused.

"I want to know," Marshall continued in his statement, "why the Navy disregarded official warnings by the San Francisco waterfront unions—before the Port Chicago disaster—that an explosion was inevitable if they persisted in using untrained seamen in the loading of ammunition. I want to know why the Navy disregarded an offer by these same unions to send experienced men to train Navy personnel in the safe handling of explosives. . . . I want to know why the commissioned officers at Port Chicago were allowed to race their men. I want to know why bets ranging from $5 up were made between division officers as to whose crew would load more ammunition."

Marshall also wanted to know why other men who refused to load ammunition were not charged, including one hundred men from the First Division who he said refused to work even before August 9 and then were quietly shipped overseas. No mention of these men was ever officially made, he said.

Marshall's questions were not merely rhetorical; he was planning to seriously press for answers to them.

Meanwhile, on Treasure Island the trial was winding to a conclusion as the prosecution called rebuttal witnesses to undermine the defense case. The rebuttal, however, did not go all that well. Several of the officers who took the men's statements at Camp Shoemaker ran into trouble under cross-examination by Lieutenant Veltmann. Lieutenant William Johnson admitted that he put in the statements what he thought was important for his report to Judge Advocate Coakley.

"If a man said he was afraid to handle ammunition, you didn't put that in, did you?" Veltmann queried.

"No, sir."

Another Shoemaker lieutenant, Patrick Gilmore, an intelligence officer who interrogated the men, testified that no threats were used against the men, but he said he did not inform the men they could refuse to make a statement if they did not wish to do so. He admitted that the statements were not complete; that he put in their statements only "what I thought was germane." Lieutenant Jesse Rodriguez said that no threats were used against the men, but Veltmann got him to admit that a marine guard armed with a revolver was sometimes present during the interrogations.

Ensign Leslie Walden, assigned to something called the Negro Rotation Program at Camp Shoemaker, interviewed seven of the defendants. He admitted that although all of them said they were afraid of ammunition, that remark found its way into only one of the written statements he prepared. He said that he, like others of the interrogators, was looking for material that pertained to the so-called "don't work" list and the meeting on the barge.

On the last day of testimony in the trial, Thursday, October 19, 1944, Lieutenant John Colombo declared that some of the men appeared confused about whether they could be charged with mutiny when he interviewed them. He said some apparently believed that only if sailors forcibly took possession of a ship from its commanding officers could they be so charged.

They were mistaken.

CHAPTER

9

Closing Arguments and Verdict

THE SUMMATIONS

There was no session in the trial on Friday, but on Saturday, October 21, Judge Advocate Coakley made the closing argument for the prosecution. Coakley's approach was to present a narrative of events from the explosion in July through the work stoppage in August, which he said added up to conspiracy and mutiny.

As soon as the men arrived at Camp Shoemaker after the explosion there was mutinous talk among them. Men from different divisions were mixed together for a day or two. It was at Shoemaker, Coakley contended, that the mutiny started brewing. "The talk about refusing to work, the talk about getting thirty days survivors' leave, the talk about getting a change of duty, transfer of base and all that sort of thing, the talk about the fear of ammunition and getting out of loading ammunition probably started over at Camp Shoemaker." Later, after the Fourth and Eighth Divisions were transferred to Mare Island barracks in Vallejo, threats were made against men who didn't want to go along with the work stoppage,

Coakley continued, and lists began to circulate in both divisions; conspiratorial meetings were held in the barracks. In the Second Division there was also mutinous talk, he said.

In what he called the second phase of the case, beginning with the work stoppage on August 9, Coakley argued that the men who balked were later given direct orders to load ammunition and refused to do so. The mutinous conspiracy continued on the barge when Joe Small urged the men to stick together. The fifty accused men, he concluded, were those who continued to hold out even after Admiral Wright gave them a final opportunity to back down on August 11.

In his final comments prosecutor Coakley reminded the court of his definition of mutiny: "Collective insubordination, collective disobedience of lawful orders of a superior officer, is mutiny. A conspiracy to disobey the lawful orders of a superior is mutiny."

"There is a war on," the prosecutor appealed to the court. "There was an ammunition ship to be loaded . . . and fear was no excuse. Under the circumstances I cannot understand how any man in the uniform could be so depraved mentally as to come into a court of law in a time of war and under oath say, 'I was afraid to handle ammunition.' A man . . . who is so depraved as to say that is capable of giving testimony that is false. . . . And what kind of discipline, what kind of morale would we have if men in the United States Navy could refuse to obey an order and then get off on the grounds of fear?"

The defense strategy, in its closing argument, was to deny that there was a mutinous conspiracy and instead to argue that the men were in a state of shock; that fear caused by the explosion was behind their reluctance to return to ammunition handling. "These fifty men had been at Port Chicago for from three to twenty-five months prior to the date of the explosion," defense attorney Veltmann said in his summation on Monday, October 23. "They had loaded ammunition, handling all types of explosives, large and small, in their daily work. . . . They were all subjected to the danger and the uncertainty of that work without an opportunity to fight back when and if the danger should rear its head and strike without warning, and strike without warning it did on the 17th of July. . . . The repercussions from that catastrophe linger in this court today—the damage wrought by that explosion is well known and the lives lost have been counted as a matter of public knowledge. The confusion, the terror and shock were new experiences to these men and one they could not know was coming. When you cannot see or hear the danger until after it bursts in your face, until after the flames envelop your surroundings, until after the concussion has shaken your world and wiped out the lives of your fellow workers without warning, when you see them picked up in baskets and pieces—an arm, a leg, or a head and shoulder—or you help pick up the remnants of human bodies, as some of these men did, when you can't see or hear your opponent in battle you must fear him—fear him the more for the reason he can wipe your name from the slate of life with one sweep and you are powerless to resist his move. Certainly, genuine fear can be engendered from the type of duty that these men had—without undergoing the experience of a blast practically unprecedented in history. Certainly, fear is the logical result of such an experience, an uncontrollable fear, a fear actually that controls your actions and influences your normal reasoning beyond your ability to handle it."

With regard to the prosecution charge that there had been mutinous talk among the men prior to the August 9 work refusal, the defense responded: "There was talk of ammunition at Shoemaker, so the prosecution insists—yes, there probably was, but there is no reliable recorded evidence of the type of talk that the prosecution would have you believe took place. There was no talk of refusing to load ammunition; there was no talk of joining minds and forces to usurp, subvert, or override superior military authority. If there was conversation among the men, it must have been of the specific incident of the explosion. The damage that it took and the fear that it imposed in the minds of the men, as individuals—what would be more natural than for these men and others in their division to exchange comments along these lines? Have you ever discussed with a friend, with whom you witnessed an unusual scene or accident, the details involved? Did you exchange opinions as to how it might have happened; didn't you gentlemen, in fact, discuss with your acquaintances the explosion at Port Chicago? I did—and I feel certain that you have done the same. And what would be more natural than the discussion and exchange of views by the men that underwent that experience? That is not conspiracy; that is not scheming; that does not provide the essential elements of mutiny or conspiracy; nor even lay the groundwork therefore."

As to the list or lists that were circulated, Veltmann replied that the men were simply exercising their right to petition for a change of duty. "What was the list for? It was a list of men who didn't want to handle ammunition, and can you wonder at that? The evidence on that matter points to the fact that the list was to be handed to Lieutenant Delucchi, the division officer of the Fourth Division. . . . Now I ask you if this is true—and it must be, for therein lies the only reason for the existence of any such paper— would the men who intended to present their desires to their division officer through the list place anything on the list, or originate it for a purpose that would be contrary to the existence of such a list itself—and by labeling the list with the statement that it contained the names of men afraid of ammunition and those desiring a change of duty, those not wanting to handle ammunition—are such men guilty of conspiracy to mutiny, or were they following what they had known to be the democratic way of life which incorporates the right to petition and freedom of expression of desires?"

Finally, as to the prosecution contention that the August 10 meeting on the barge was a mutinous conspiracy led by Joe Small, Veltmann answered: "Yes, Small talked at that meeting, apparently he was the only one and the meeting lasted at the outset from four to five minutes. . . . Small talked for a few minutes and in so doing fulfilled what he considered his duty and responsibility under legitimate appointment by superior authority." Veltmann argued that Small called the meeting to keep order and maintain discipline. "And it is submitted that the meeting on the barge at which Small urged cooperation and observation of the rules under which the men lived was greatly responsible for the highly acceptable order and discipline that was maintained."

From the outset of the court-martial proceeding the defense strongly objected to the mutiny charge, pointing out that the legal definition of mutiny was a concerted effort to usurp, subvert, or override military authority. The defense contended that there had been no such attempt in this case—that the men were orderly and obeyed all orders, with the exception of orders to load ammunition. On this latter point the defense also argued that no direct orders to load ammunition were ever issued, at least not to all the accused men. Even if such orders were issued, the defense argued, refusal to obey an order does not constitute mutiny.

In essence, the defense position was that the work stoppage was due to an aggregate of actions by individuals who acted out of fear because of their common experience of the explosion at Port Chicago. There was no deliberate conspiracy to usurp, subvert, or override military authority. The prosecution, on the other hand, argued that testimony about the men talking of not returning to work prior to August 9, and the barge meeting on August 10 at which Joe Small spoke, was evidence of a deliberate conspiracy to mutiny. Moreover, the fact that all of the men refused to return to work more or less simultaneously was further evidence of intentional collective resistance. Collective insubordination is mutiny, Coakley concluded.

As the trial went into its final days the accused men reflected upon their fate. They were not optimistic. "The trial was just procedure," one of them said later.

"We knew before the trial's end what it was going to be like. We knew we was going to be found guilty, no matter what we said, because we were told that we couldn't say certain things or that it had been covered, and you knew full well it wasn't covered." Commenting on the defense strategy, Joe Small said: "I think they tried to show me as a dedicated Navy man and the rest of them [the accused] as inexperienced boys, and me trying to control them in the best way I knew how. But they admitted that we were going to get some time, because it is a written law that you don't get away with nothing in the Navy. Regardless of your defense, you can expect to be found guilty."

Other defendants feared that they would be found guilty and then sentenced to be shot.

THE VERDICT

The mutiny trial had taken thirty-two days of hearings—six weeks in all—and it had generated more than fourteen hundred pages of transcript in seven volumes. Yet, on Tuesday afternoon, October 24, the thirty-third day of the trial, after only eighty minutes of deliberation by the members of Osterhaus's court—presumably including time for lunch, as the decision was made during the noon break—all fifty of the defendants were found guilty of making a mutiny. As Thurgood Marshall observed, this averaged out to about a minute and a half of deliberation for each defendant.

The trial board did not immediately announce the sentences, as they were to be first reviewed by higher military authority. However, the court had sentenced all of the men to fifteen years in prison. Joe Small and all the other men received the identical sentence: "The court . . . sentences him, Joseph R. Small, seaman first class, U.S. Naval Reserve, to be reduced to the rating of apprentice seaman, to be confined for a period of fifteen years, then to be dishonorably discharged from the United States naval service, and to suffer all the accessories of said sentence. . . ."

The swiftness of the verdict and the uniformity of the sentences left little doubt that the court members had much earlier made up their minds that the men were guilty en masse. The court refused to see the fifty men individually or recognize that there were major differences in the circumstances of each man. The board did meet later to consider evidence of mitigation, but only seventeen-year-old John Dunn, because of his youth, was recommended for clemency.

The court's findings were sent to Admiral Wright for review. The following month, on November 15, Wright reduced sentences, but not for all of the men. Twenty-four of the men, including Jack Crittenden, Charles Gray, and Cyril Sheppard, had their sentences reduced to twelve years imprisonment. Another group of eleven men, including Edward Longmire and Julius Dixson, had their sentences reduced to ten years. Sentences for the five youngest men with the shortest periods of service were reduced to eight years imprisonment. John Dunn and Martin Bordenave were in this group. But the fifteen-year sentences for ten of the men— including Joe Small, Alphonso McPherson, Ollie Green, and Frank Henry—were allowed to stand. For most of the men even the reduced sentences meant that they were facing a term of imprisonment half as long as they had already lived. All were still to be dishonorably discharged after serving their sentences.

Meanwhile, the other 208 men who initially joined the work refusal were given summary court-martials and each sentenced to a bad conduct discharge and three months' forfeiture of pay.

With perverse but unrelenting logic those who were responsible for the conditions at Port Chicago were never accused of any wrongdoing, while those who were the chief victims of those conditions were charged, tried, convicted, and jailed.

By the end of November, the fifty men were incarcerated at the Terminal Island Disciplinary Barracks in San Pedro, near Los Angeles.

At the Terminal Island prison the men were divided into groups of five or six and placed in different barracks with other prisoners. But the Port Chicago men were assigned to work details together, and the harrowing experiences which they had endured over the preceding months forged a group consciousness among them that set them off from the other prisoners. "We stuck together," Edward Waldrop recalled. "That bunch of men stuck together better than any bunch of blacks I've ever seen. Very seldom would one get out of line. We had talked it over, and we knew that if one did something, then we all suffer."

Joe Small remembered how the other prisoners and guards reacted to them: "In the time that we were confined at San Pedro we never had any trouble of any major kind. We used to get into a lot of junk between ourselves, some fights, stuff like that, but we were a separated group. Nobody bother us and we didn't bother nobody. We had our own work details that kept us together. They used to refer to us as the Port Chicago Boys. We had a reputation for being unruly and bad, and therefore we had very little trouble."

The trouble was in the situation itself rather than in the responses of the guards and other prisoners. They had gotten out of Port Chicago only to face a long imprisonment at Terminal Island. They knew the NAACP had gotten involved and planned to appeal their convictions, but for most of them this held out little hope.

CHAPTER

10

Appeal and Release

The mutiny trial was widely covered by the local San Francisco Bay Area press, wire services, and nationally circulated black newspapers such as the *Chicago Defender* and the *Pittsburgh Courier*. The trial and conviction were greeted with indignation by black leaders. "The Negro people are well aware of the pattern of discrimination practiced by the Navy," said Joseph James, president of the San Francisco branch of the NAACP, "and they are very much concerned about this trial. I feel that a general investigation of the policies which led up to this thing should be made at once." James's comments were echoed by others. "I don't condone an act of mutiny against the government in time of war," declared prominent Oakland attorney J. C. Henderson, "yet I feel that the discriminatory policy of the Navy and the overall conditions to which the boys on trial have been subjected should be considered before ipso facto condemning them as traitors."

The sudden expansion of military and industrial facilities in the Bay Area during the war had led to a dramatic increase in the black population of the region betwen 1940 and 1944. San Francisco's black population alone grew from less than 5,000 to more than 12,000 in this period; shipyard towns such as Vallejo and Richmond experienced an even larger growth. With the increase in the black population came an increase in acts of overt racial discrimination against the new immigrants, especially in housing and employment. The first ghettoes appeared, and black shipyard workers found themselves being segregated by the boilermakers' union. By 1944, said Joseph James, the local NAACP branch found itself carrying "the burden of protest and representation for the Negro community." That the NAACP Legal Defense Fund came to represent the Port Chicago men in their legal appeal was almost inevitable.

During his twelve days attending the mutiny trial, Thurgood Marshall began formulating a plan for an appeal campaign. He conferred with the men themselves, his colleagues in the NAACP, and others familiar with Navy practices. Marshall himself blasted the trial in the November issue of *Crisis* magazine published by the NAACP. He charged that the defendants were being tried for mutiny "solely because of their race and color." He described the case as "one of the worst 'frame-ups' we have come across in a long time. It was deliberately planned and staged by certain officers to discredit Negro seamen."

While attending the trial Marshall also met Mary Lindsay, a white reporter for the left-wing *Peoples World* newspaper. Lindsay had written carefully and extensively on the trial. Her sympathetic coverage impressed Marshall. Subsequently he arranged for her to write a pamphlet about the case for the NAACP Legal Defense Fund. It was a copy of this pamphlet—published without Mary Lindsay's byline in 1945—that caught my attention more than thirty years later.

(Mary Lindsay committed suicide in a hotel in 1972. The hotel owner remembered her as a pleasant woman who paid her rent in advance when she checked into the hotel. She then went to her room and took an overdose of sleeping pills. No one could say why Mary Lindsay committed suicide or why she chose the Leamington Hotel in Oakland as the place of her death, except that this was the hotel in which she had stayed when she covered the mutiny trial in 1944.)

Upon his return to New York after the trial, Marshall fired off a letter to Secretary of the Navy Forrestal. He commended the naval defense team for good work in defending the accused men "within the limitations of Navy rules." But Marshall knew very well that the men's grievances had not been presented at the trial, and he proceeded to outline some of these in his letter to Forrestal in the form of questions, much like those in his earlier statement in California calling for an investigation of the Navy. Marshall asked why only blacks were assigned to loading ammunition at Port Chicago; why they were not given training for ammunition handling; why they were subjected to forced competition by the officers; why they could not be promoted to better ratings; and why they were not given survivors' leaves after the explosion, among other questions.

Forrestal refused to respond to the questions on training and competition on the grounds that the facts had not been established. As to discrimination, he replied disingenuously that since Port Chicago was manned predominantly by black enlisted personnel, then "naturally, therefore, the only Naval personnel loading ammunition regularly were Negroes." He said there were other ammunition depots manned by white personnel. If there is discrimination, he wrote, it must be against whites as well as blacks. As for the lack of ratings, Forrestal described the men's tenure at Port Chicago as a "trial period . . . during which the men considered most capable of assuming added responsibilities can be selected." He gave no example of any such selection process ever having taken place.

Finally, with regard to the lack of survivors' leaves, Forrestal asserted that previous experience had shown that "requiring men to immediately return to handling ammunition, after an explosion, is the preferred method of preventing them from building up mental and emotional barriers which, if allowed to accumulate, become increasingly difficult to overcome."

Forrestal sought to liquidate the question of racial discrimination in the Navy semantically. But the explosion and the ensuing publicity about the work force at Port Chicago had touched a nerve. Moreover, 1944 was a presidential election year and the Roosevelt administration was eagerly courting the black vote. Memoranda circulating in the Navy Department expressed concern about possible adverse reaction to the discrimination issue, and as early as September 1944 orders had gone out requiring the formation of two white loading divisions to work at Port Chicago and Mare

Island. Thus, while Forrestal tried to evade the discrimination issue his staff was taking steps to neutralize criticism. But they acted too late.

The explosion and the highly publicized trial focused public attention on racial discrimination in the Navy and provoked an angry outcry from the black community and liberal white groups throughout the country. The protest began spontaneously as a few people, learning of the trial, wrote letters objecting to the treatment of the accused men and the sentences given them. Sensing the importance of the case, the NAACP Legal Defense Fund in December 1944 began making plans to enter the case. A two-pronged strategy was worked out. First, a campaign would be mounted to publicize the case, making use of Mary Lindsay's pamphlet to build popular support for the release of the men; second, the NAACP Legal Defense Fund, after obtaining written permission from the defendants to do so, would actively intercede on behalf of the men and file an appeal brief when the case came up for review before the Judge Advocate General of the Navy in Washington.

Beginning in January 1945 editorials on the case appeared in *Crisis* magazine and other black publications. Over the next several months thousands of names were collected on petitions, labor and civil liberties organizations issued statements, protest meetings were held, and prominent individuals, including Eleanor Roosevelt, were enlisted in the effort to have the convictions reversed.

Eleanor Roosevelt had learned of the work refusal incident in September 1944 when the President passed along to her the report he received on the matter from Forrestal. She returned the report without written comment, but in April 1945 she sent Forrestal a copy of the NAACP's "Mutiny" pamphlet. With the pamphlet she included a note saying, "I hope in the case of these boys special care will be taken." She gave as the reason for her concern the rather patronizing explanation that "I think they suffer more than other people from frustration in childhood which makes it difficult for them to take the ordinary things that we all expect people to take in life." Being traumatized by a massive explosion hardly seemed like an ordinary thing that we are all expected to take in life, but perhaps Mrs. Roosevelt thought her reasoning the best way to appeal to Secretary Forrestal's compassion.

Eleanor Roosevelt's was one voice among the many who joined in the campaign on behalf of the convicted Port Chicago seamen.

The campaign continued throughout 1945 and found support in many different regions of the country.

Thurgood Marshall drafted an appeal brief, and on April 3 he made a personal appearance at the Navy's Judge Advocate General's office in Washington to present his arguments. Marshall contended that no direct order to load ammunition was given to the fifty defendants, and that there was no mutiny even if an order was given. ("I can't understand why, whenever more than one Negro disobeys an order, it is mutiny," he complained.) Finally, he accused prosecutor Coakley of deliberately misleading the court on the law of mutiny, and of introducing inadmissible hearsay evidence. "The accused were made scapegoats in a situation brought about by a combination of circumstances," Marshall wrote in the brief. "Justice can only be done in this case by a complete reversal of the findings."

But the findings were not reversed; the convictions were upheld. The Secretary of the Navy's office sent a memo to Admiral Wright in May advising that the admission of hearsay evidence had been an error in the trial. Wright was instructed to have the court reconvene and reconsider its findings after "wholly disregarding" the hearsay testimony. Admiral Osterhaus duly called the board back together, and on June 12, 1945, the court announced that it refused to budge an inch, sticking to its original guilty verdicts and sentences in the case of all fifty of the defendants. Admiral Wright, in turn, reaffirmed his reductions of sentence for some of the men.

The NAACP urged its members and supporters to redouble their efforts during that summer and send another wave of protest letters to the Navy.

With the Japanese surrender after the atomic bombing of Hiroshima and Nagasaki in August 1945 (the nuclear bomb dropped on Hiroshima was shipped out via Port Chicago) the war hysteria abated. The severe sentences in the mutiny case no longer appeared justified. Moreover, according to a memo sent by a Captain H. E. Stassen to Secretary Forrestal, the case had made its point of underscoring "the continuous emphasis of military discipline upon labor battalions." The mutiny trial had been a warning to other dissident servicemen. Now, with the war won, the Navy could back away from the heavy-handed sentences. In September the Navy lopped off another year from all the sentences, and the following month Captain Stassen recommended that sentences be reduced to two years for men with good conduct records, and three years for each of the other convicted men, with credit for time already served. (Stassen was Harold E. Stassen, the former governor of Minnesota who would later become a perennial liberal candidate for President.)

Meanwhile, instances of mass resistance such as the Port Chicago rebellion, the Guam riot, and the Seabees protests against discrimination had persuaded some of the Navy bureaucracy that Jim Crow was an unwise policy, not necessarily because of its unjustness and economic inefficiency, but as much because it concentrated blacks together in groups and made collective action by black servicemen possible. Better to disperse black sailors in the Navy by mixing them in with whites. Navy officials who in the past had opposed racial integration now found themselves advocates of this "enlightened" new policy.

Starting in late 1944, under Forrestal's guidance, steps toward desegregation were taken. That October the Bureau of Personnel lifted restrictions, with some exceptions, on the use of black personnel and allowed commanders "to assign Negroes . . . to such activities, and in such numbers, as they see fit." Over the next year integrated crews, but with the black complement limited initially to no more than ten percent, were introduced on some auxiliary vessels. Meanwhile, orders went out to limit the number of black personnel at ammunition depots to thirty percent of the total, in keeping with the Navy's new policy "to assure . . . a representative cross-section of Naval personnel at all activities."

To prepare its officers for the new era of integration, the Navy, early in 1945, issued a "Guide to the Command of Negro Naval Personnel." This fifteen-page booklet informed its readers that "the Navy accepts no theories of racial differences in inborn ability," although "it is recognized, of course, that Negro performance in Naval training and tasks . . . has not been equal to the average performance of white personnel." Proper training, the guide advised, could overcome the "handicaps" under which Negroes labored. It urged officers (assumed to be white, of course) to make no distinction based on color in the treatment of naval personnel; blacks were to be rated, and promoted, on the same basis as whites. Officers were further warned against referring to blacks as "nigger." "The terms 'boy,' 'darkey,' 'coon,' 'jig,' 'uncle,' 'Negress,' and 'your people' are also resented," the guide authoritatively stated. Even compliments might be misunderstood, it concluded, and officers should not go out of their way to ask their Negro personnel to do any tap dancing, guitar playing, or singing of spirituals.

In June 1945 the Navy announced that it was discontinuing segregation in training camps and other programs. To herald its new policy, the Navy borrowed Lester Granger, the black executive director of the National Urban League, a moderate civil rights group, to become special advisor to the Secretary of the Navy. In this capacity Granger made three tours of Navy bases in the United States and overseas, including Port Chicago. A graduate of Dartmouth College, like Forrestal, Granger talked with thousands of black seamen and their officers. In November Granger made his report and recommendations. He noted instances of continuing discrimination, but overall he praised the Navy, declaring that "the Navy means business about revising its racial policy and making it possible for every member of the service to give his best efforts in his nation's cause without hinder and without discrimination." In special reports on the Port Chicago and Guam cases, Granger urged the Navy to relax the sentences imposed.

Two months later, in January 1946, the Secretary of the Navy's office announced that forty-seven of the Port Chicago men were being released from prison. (Two remained for a time in the prison hospital and a third was not released because of a bad conduct record.) With the war over, some seventeen hundred imprisoned servicemen were given clemency, including the Guam and Port Chicago groups.

The Port Chicago men were released from prison but not from the Navy. They were divided into small groups and then sent overseas to the South Pacific for a "probationary period." Finally, over the course of the following months, the men made their way back and returned to their families and their private lives in the United States.

Joe Small recalled this time of exile, of wandering back and forth across the Pacific Ocean, and the irony of the new policy of racial integration.

"They picked us out in groups of five and they put us on board different ships and shipped us out. My group went aboard a ship one night about ten and were assigned our bunks and went to bed. The next morning when I woke up I detected the motion of the ship. So I got up and went on deck and I didn't see land anyplace.

I said to one of the sailors, 'How far are we from the nearest land?' He said about two miles. We were completely out of sight of land, so I asked which way. He said, 'Straight down.' We had a big laugh about it.

"We rode. We had no duties, nothing to do but make mess call, roam about the ship, and sleep. We rode and rode, just back and forth from one port to another. We never left the ship. Just on the ship all the time. They said they were conditioning us for discharge.

"We wound up back at Treasure Island for a long time. Then they gave us a ship to Seattle, Washington. I was the first black seaman that a lot of these white fellows ever saw. I had a lot of conflict over that. They expected me to be a steward's mate. I was on board this ship to Seattle and there was this young shavetail lieutenant from Massachusetts and he gave me the job of relaying orders. I would stand on the fantail with earphones on and receive the orders from the bridge and then repeat the orders to the crew. When we were casting off he would say, 'Cast off one!' and I'd repeat, 'Cast off one!'—and these white boys were pulling on this big red line. I was standing up there giving them orders; it caused quite a commotion.

"There was a bos'n's mate there from Alabama—big, red-headed fellow. I used to eat with the stewards; they would get their tray and the officers' trays and go upstairs. But one day the lieutenant told me, 'Small, you eat downstairs with the crew.' I said, 'Look, there'll be trouble if I eat down there.' 'You eat down there and I'll take care of the trouble.'

"Sure enough, the first day I walked into the mess hall and sat down to eat, this big Southerner sat down opposite me. He said, 'By Gawd, this the first time I ever ate with a nigger.' I had a mug of coffee, a Navy mug with no handles. I dashed the coffee in his face, and then hit him with the mug. Before he could get straightened out I was across the table on him.

"At the time I weighed about 155 pounds, and he must have weighed 240, but I was too fast for him to hit me. I was also too light to hurt him. I would hit him but I couldn't hurt him. He'd swing at me but he couldn't hit me. So finally the lieutenant came in and broke it up. He talked to us and we shook hands.

"This Southerner and I became best of friends. Everywhere I went he was with me. We would go into a bar and he'd say, 'Give me two beers.' They'd set up one beer and he'd slide me the beer.

Then he'd say, 'Now give me a beer.' They'd say, 'We don't serve niggers in here.' And we'd tear the bar up. We'd turn over tables and everything.

"One day I asked him, 'Alex, why you like me so?' He said, 'Small, you're a man. I found out something. I used to think that all black people carried knives and guns and razors. I kept expecting you to pull out a razor, but you fought me with your fists. You knew you had no chance to win, but still you fought me with your fists. I got respect for you; I like you.'

"None of this was ever publicized."

CHAPTER

11

Conclusion

The Port Chicago rebellion was a crucible. It was a searing test of the character of the enlisted men who became involved in the work stoppage. They faced double jeopardy: to go back to work was dangerous and unacceptable, but to refuse to work was to risk imprisonment and even death. They believed that their hope lay in a collective refusal to work, yet collective action could be, and was, construed as mutiny. The men grappled with this terrible dilemma and were torn by conflicting hopes and fears as they struggled to forge a response to what had become an intolerable situation. Each had to decide not once but several times whether to resist or to capitulate. In effect, the Port Chicago rebellion was an attempt to transform an aggregate of individuals into a self-conscious collectivity. It was a spontaneous strike that threatened to become a full-scale resistance movement.

Today the remaining survivors of the Port Chicago disaster are living quiet lives—some still working, some unemployed, some retired. Many others are dead. Those still living are in their sixties and seventies. The men I interviewed have complex feelings about the work stoppage. Several men expressed pride at their act of resistance and the fact that the fifty accused men stuck together throughout the ordeal of trial and imprisonment. Others were more circumspect, voicing concern about possible negative repercussions to themselves or their families even at this late date.

The Port Chicago men were finally discharged from the Navy "under honorable conditions," but the mutiny convictions still stand. In 1977 one of the men, Martin Bordenave, enlisted the services of NAACP representative Marion Hill in an attempt to get the case reopened and the men's names cleared. Their effort was unsuccessful.

Joe Small was discharged from the Navy in July 1946. Presently he lives with his family in a New Jersey town. More than forty years have passed since the rebellion by the Port Chicago men. How does he feel about what happened so long ago? Is he angry with the Navy for its treatment of the work refusers? What has his life been like since leaving the Navy? What would he tell his sons about the Navy? What meaning has he found in his experiences? One day as we talked he ruminated on these and other questions.

That work stoppage was inevitable. It would have happened. But something else had to happen to give it a shove. The explosion was the instrument by which all of this injustice was brought to light. Had the explosion not happened, 320 men would not have lost their lives, but eventually something would have happened to bring about this work stoppage—that the conditions might be exposed.

It just so happens that the explosion came about and that was the opportunity for us to realize that what we were in fear of all the time came true. Now you want me to go back to the same thing I was doing under the same conditions and open myself up to the possibility of the same thing happening again, and I may not escape this time.

So my only way of changing that is to not work. It wasn't a planned thing; it was just brought on by circumstances, working conditions—it was inevitable. Just the same way the explosion was inevitable. Something would have happened to set off that explosion because of the way they were handling that ammunition, it had to happen. What else can I say? It's been more than forty years ago, but that is more vivid in my memory than the actual court-martial—the conditions under which we were working, because they were appalling. That's what we were trying to get out of, but we had no way to get out of it. The explosion was an avenue of escape, and I think it would have been stupid to say to that man, "Yes, I'll go back to work." Knowing that conditions were the same, the officers were the same, the dangers of what happened were the same, I had to say no. It was the only way to change it.

We expected to be asked to return to duty after the explosion 'cause that was the only thing we knew to do. Since we weren't qualified seamen we had no expectations of going to sea. We weren't cooks, we weren't bakers, we weren't stewards. The only thing we knew was handling ammunition, and we fully expected to be asked to go back to the same work. And the men had made up their minds themselves that they weren't going to do it. That was the general situation. They got me involved in it only because the officer directed his question to me. If he had not called any particular name I would never have been involved in it in that respect. But he said, "Small, front and center! Will you return to duty?" I said no. Then someone over in the ranks said, "If Small don't go, we ain't going either." That put me out in the front.

I had a personal meeting with one of the commanding officers, and he riled me. He told me, "If you don't go back to duty I'm gonna have you shot." I told him, "You bald-headed so-and-so, go ahead and shoot me!" I regretted having said it, but what they expected me to do was to just go back to duty and forget everything. They assumed that if I went back to duty everybody would follow me. But I had what I considered a legitimate reason for not going back to work: the danger in working.

As for the trial, I always knew that the verdict was mandatory. The Navy could come up with it regardless of what was brought out during the trial or what testimony was brought out, the verdict would have been the same. Not because the verdict would have been justified, but because it was the only way to save face.

I had a dream one night before the trial, and in that dream I was told that I was going to jail. Well, it was a dream, and I interpreted the dream as meaning that. I saw a snake and that snake bit me, and I was wounded. But the wound healed. There was always a scar there, but the wound, the pain, was gone. The next morning when I awoke I called Miller and I told him about the dream. He said, "Well, what does it mean?" And I said, "We're going to jail, but we won't stay: they'll let us out, and we'll go back to duty. We'll always have this mark against us, but it won't bother us in civilian life."

When I finally came back home from the service, my brother, the one next to me, was married and had a family. My baby brother was soon to marry and have a family. My sister had married and she was living in Boston. It left just me and my mother at home. Then she left in 1946, the year I came out of the service. My sister had moved to Chicago and her husband was sick; my mother went to Chicago to spend some time with her. Her husband died, and my mother stayed in Chicago. She died in Chicago in 1961.

I got married to Louise Johnson in 1947. I had seen her before I went into the service, but she was only a young girl. In fact, when I met her after I came out of the service I didn't know who she was. I still had my uniform on when I met her. Coming from the ball park, that's when I met her. We had a couple of dates and got to talking and I realized I had seen her before. But she must have been about fourteen or fifteen then, and she was nineteen when I came out of the service. We went together for eight months, then we got married. I came out of the service in July; we got married in April '47.

I built a house on the old family place, but it burned down in '58. I lost two boys. One of the twins—I had twin boys and I lost one of the twins—and an albino boy. After the fire we moved in with my in-laws.

I was in debt. I was so deep in debt that I couldn't borrow any money to rebuild. When the house burned down I only had construction insurance on it. That only paid off the bills I owed on the house. It left me with the ground, but it didn't pay off all the bills I owed. So I sold the property in order to settle up my debts, and we bought this place in '61. I bought with the intention of building on it, but the political machine changed right after I bought it and they wouldn't let me build on it. [The Smalls live on the ground floor of an uncompleted building that was originally intended to be a multistory dwelling.] The governing body changed from Democrat to Republican and they rezoned this district, "No Multiple Dwellings."

That stopped me up until two years ago. Then they would've given me a permit to build, but I had to move everything upstairs and make a cellar down here. I didn't see where it was feasible to spend $20,000 once to build up, and then pull $20,000 out from down here. So I never built. I think it's a little too late for me to start building now, so I'm just going to tough it out here. It's comfortable. It needs repairing—that last winter really did me in as far as my roof is concerned, and my ceilings. There was a storm here year before last, a big storm, flooded Trenton. That storm ripped my roof off, and I haven't stopped it from leaking since. But with the help of the Lord I'll get it straightened out this year, get it back to like it was for next winter.

I was in the Baptist Church before I went into the service and I went back into my church after I came out. I remained in the Baptist Church until 1960 when all that changed. With the advent of the Holy Ghost into my life it all changed. I left the Baptist Church and joined the Apostolic Church. Certain things went on in the Baptist Church that I knew were not in keeping with God's will. The pastor we had preached against alcohol, but he kept alcohol in his study. He preached against adultery and fornication, yet on several instances he was caught in the act.

My oldest son went into the Navy right after he graduated from high school. Though he was raised in the church, when he came back after four years in the Navy he was an agnostic. "Show me!" he said. "Lester, you were raised in this." "Yeah, but I don't believe it." The Muslims got to him in the service. He was asked to accept a discharge because of his subversive actions in the military. In contrast with my situation in the military, he just objected to the white man. Period. He didn't want a white man to ask him his name because he was convinced that, first, the white man is the devil incarnate and second, the white man wrote the Bible to keep the black man in slavery. Third thing, the black man would never progress in any way as long as he was subject to the will of the white man. Lester came back from the Navy with this "Kill the white man" attitude. He objected to the white man so much that he wouldn't even speak to him.

It's totally objective to me, because by one blood God created all men. That is the Bible. If I didn't believe that then I wouldn't believe anything in the Bible. By one blood God created all men. Lester's views have changed, since I've been able to talk to him and live a life in front of him. But when he first came home, if a white boy said, "Hi, Lester," he was ready to fight.

I don't find nothing wrong with the Navy as a whole, because the Navy has changed tremendously since I was in there. There's been tremendous strides toward desegregation. My other son here is going into the Navy next month. I wouldn't want him to go into any service except the Navy. In the Navy, even though he is discriminated against, he will get good meals, he will get a bed to sleep in every night, and he will be where he can get medical attention. There's no war going on, so even if he does go overseas he won't go into combat. He'll be given a chance to get a higher education or he'll be taught a trade he can use in civilian life. I just like the Navy, even though it was rough when I was in there. I didn't have so hard a time that I carry a grudge against the Navy. I still respect the Navy, and I still think that out of the three military branches the Navy's the best.

When I came out of the service I just started building. I'm handy with tools. I built my first house from a chicken coop into a seven-room split-level. People saw my ability in doing my own work, and they got me to do work for them. Eventually the work got so much that I needed a truck. When I got the truck the law stated I had to have a name on it. Instead of putting "Joe Small" on it, I put "Small Construction" on it. Then I went around doing construction work and I was able to quit the job that I had.

They kept me busy. I built a house up on Churchill Avenue. I took the blueprints to a supplier and he gave me an estimate on the materials that would go into the house. Then I figured out the labor and gave the customers a price for the house. They accepted it. I paid the supplier as I received the payments on the house. When I went down to make the final payment I owed him something like $700. He told me, "Small, you owe me $2,700." I said, "That's not in keeping with the estimate you gave me." He said, "Well, my secretary made a mistake." I said, "I'm not responsible for your secretary's mistakes." That very night I called my lawyer and had my name incorporated. The lawyer was smart enough to set the date back two days. That made the corporation come into being two days before I had the argument with the supplier; so he couldn't sue me. All he could do was sue the corporation, and the corporation had nothing. So it just died down.

That's the way I got incorporated, and I stayed incorporated for about twelve years. During this time I had all kinds of opportunities to make money, but it was often dishonest and I wouldn't take it. I could have been a contractor for the city of New Brunswick, but

I had to overbid jobs and then shove money under the table. I would never go along with it, so I seldom got any city bids. They would offer me small jobs, like putting a roof on a city-owned building. That was worth a couple of thousand dollars, and I would buy a couple of bottles of whiskey for somebody. That was all right for me but when it came down to the big money I couldn't get it because I wouldn't go along with it.

The Mafia wanted to put union men on the job. I wasn't union but they said, if you put two union men to work for you we will get you a job. The two union men would just have their names on paper and they wouldn't show up for work, but I would have to meet their payroll every week. I said, "Naw, I'm not going to do it. If you want to give me two union men that's going to work I'll pay them." They picketed my job. I got an eight-inch block and hauled it all the way to the top of a three-story building, dropped it on the sidewalk right behind a picket—I missed him about two feet. The pickets left the job and didn't come back no more.

Then they blackballed me. In New Brunswick any job that was worth anything I couldn't get. That's why I never became rich. So now I'm a fix-it man, you might call it. I'm employed by a community development program and I'm doing some remodeling of a school here. I do little odd jobs on the side, put up a fence, fix a stoop, stuff like that on the side. I'm no longer in the construction business as such.

When I still was in the business white people used to come on the job and see the truck with "Small Construction" written on it. At the bottom it said, "Owned and operated by Joseph Small." They'd come up and ask for Mr. Small. I always had white boys on my crew because I found that white boys will keep the black boys' mouths clean. You hear black boys using m-f and cursing all the time. You put one white boy among them and they'll stop it. I always kept at least one white boy in my crew. When I had fifteen men working for me I had three white boys. I tried to keep them in a ratio of one to five. Salesmen used to come on the job and look at the white boy, "Mr. Small?" I'd be standing right there alongside of him and he'd start talking to the white boy. "You Mr. Small?" "No, that's Mr. Small standing alongside of ya." They'd turn red as a beet.

Yes, sir, I've gotten a lot of phone calls from people who wanted to sell me lumber and stuff like that. We'd make a date to meet on the job or at their work site. When I'd walk up they'd say, "Who do you want to see?" I'd say, "Mr. So-and-so." They'd say, "He's busy, he's going to be tied up for a while, he has an appointment to see a Mr. Small." I'd say, "I'm Mr. Small." Then their faces would show surprise . . . they expected a white man.

But that's the way these United States are; we have to live with it. I've come to the conclusion that the only way to escape it is through God. That's the only way, 'cause the devil wants everything else. And if I go along with him I won't have to take no warm clothes when I leave here!

Joe Small, who experienced more than his share of disaster, tragedy, and hardship, is philosophical about it. He is not bitter about his misfortunes; he is at peace with himself. Not without contradictions himself, he is sadly amused by the racial blinders unwittingly worn by others.

In some ways things haven't changed all that much; prejudice and discrimination—sometimes subtle, sometimes overt—are still rife in American life. But Joe Small and the other Port Chicago men did make a difference by their action. Even in the moment of their seeming failure they compelled the Navy, however unwillingly, to revamp its racial policies.

The month after the Port Chicago men were released from prison, February 1946, the U.S. Navy eliminated, officially at least, all racial barriers in its ranks. "Effective immediately," said the announcement of the new policy, "all restrictions governing types of assignments for which Negro personnel are eligible are hereby lifted. Henceforth they shall be eligible for all types of assignments, in all ratings in all facilities and in all ships. . . . In the utilization of housing, messing, and other facilities no special or unusual provisions will be made for the accommodation of Negroes."

The Navy, which had been the most exclusionist and segregated branch of the armed services, ironically became the first to accept integration as policy. To be sure, black men remained predominantly in the messman's service for years after the war, and de facto discrimination also continued. But when President Harry S. Truman ordered the complete integration of all the Armed Forces in 1948, only the Navy could claim to be already in compliance.

The change in policy could be credited to many factors, including pressure from groups like the NAACP Legal Defense Fund and individuals like Thurgood Marshall and Lester Granger. The new political climate after the war played a part, generating popular support for change. But the rebellion by the Port Chicago seamen dramatically showed that segregation was a bankrupt policy that fueled the flames of its own destruction. The men in the ranks, whatever the specific cause, were saying "No!" Though called a mutiny, the work stoppage was a strike against segregation and dangerous working conditions. And it was not the only such strike. Clearly, the policy had to change.

As for the town of Port Chicago, it no longer exists. Although heavily damaged, the town survived the explosion and rebuilt itself. But the town's civic spirit was mortally wounded; citizens squabbled over the town's future, and many of its residents wanted out. The Navy proposed to buy the town for $20 million, although an independent appraisal put the town's value at $35 million. Some residents, including the wealthy Eunice Van Winkle, who owned almost 25 percent of the town, found the Navy's plan unacceptable and sought to block it. Others were upset by what they felt was the arrogance and heavy-handedness of a Navy "land grab." Demonstrations were held in the town to protest the Navy's plan, but in 1968 the Navy prevailed, and succeeded in taking over the town completely. The Navy gained congressional authorization to buy out—or condemn—the town; subsequently Port Chicago was razed to the ground to make room for expansion of the Navy base. All that remains of Port Chicago today is the outline of the town's streets in the grassy buffer zone that surrounds the base, a silent reminder of a community that was literally consumed by the military.

In the 1960s and 1970s the Navy base was massively involved in shipping ammunition and bombs to American forces in Vietnam. The loading was now done by civilian workers. Over a hundred thousand tons of munitions passed through the facility each month. As the unpopular Vietnam War escalated, the base also became a target for antiwar demonstrations, some of which drew national attention.

In 1980 the Port Chicago base came into the news again. Now incorporated into the Concord Naval Weapons Station, it was the subject of an award-winning documentary film, *Broken Arrow*, produced by investigative reporter Stephen Talbot and aired on public television. Talbot charged that the base had become a nuclear weapons storage and transshipment facility. Nuclear bombs are routinely flown by helicopter, he asserted, over heavily populated areas from the Alameda Naval Station near Oakland to Concord, where they are stored in bunkers that are visible from the nearby highway. Talbot reported evidence of unsafe procedures being employed in the handling of the nuclear weapons. The Navy refused to confirm or deny Talbot's report. Needless to say, a disaster at a nuclear weapons facility would make the Port Chicago explosion look like a firecracker by comparison.

For me Port Chicago became more than a site of historical interest as the resurgent antiwar activism of the 1980s propelled a thousand demonstrators, myself included, to blockade the Concord/Port Chicago naval base in June 1987. The purpose of the demonstration was to protest the shipment of arms from the base to U.S.-backed counterrevolutionaries in Nicaragua and El Salvador. The demonstrators were also protesting the use of the base for nuclear weapons. In a gesture meant to honor the Port Chicago men who died in the explosion while serving their country, several of us wore T-shirts that read, "Remember Port Chicago."

Almost 250 of the protestors were arrested, and in an unexpected linking of the present with the past, those arrested were detained briefly in temporary jails that were dilapidated old Navy trailers with built-in wooden benches and metal handrails—the "cattle cars" used to transport Port Chicago ammunition loaders to the docks. As I sat talking with friends in a Navy trailer, waiting to be processed out, I felt for a moment an emotional connection with the Port Chicago "mutineers"—a feeling of kinship, in which I recognized them as spiritual fathers of a sort. I hoped my small act of civil disobedience also honored the memory of their strike. They, too, served their country.

Day after day, week after week, the demonstrations and arrests continued. Demonstrators blockaded the entrance to the base, attempting to stop the movement of arms-laden trucks and trains. Inexorably, the confrontation moved toward an awful conclusion.

On September 1, 1987, as dozens of witnesses watched in horror, a Navy train entering the base ran over a demonstrator, cutting off both his legs at the knees. The maimed man, Brian Willson, was still conscious as his wife, Holly, and fourteen-year-old stepson, Gabriel, rushed to his aid. Willson, a forty-six-year-old Vietnam veteran revulsed by the war, was part of a group of Vietnam veterans who were protesting the Reagan administration's intervention in Central America. Video footage of the incident showed that the train made no effort to slow down as it approached the blockading demonstrators. The three train crewmen, when questioned about the incident later, said they had been given a go-ahead signal by a supervisor and were under orders not to stop the train.

The incident provoked an outburst of public anger as seven thousand demonstrators gathered at the Navy base gates a few days after Willson's wounding. "When that train rolled over Brian, it rolled over all of us," said Jesse Jackson at the rally. "Brian Willson lost his legs that we might walk for justice." Some local officials called for the closing and removal of the base. But the Navy remained determined to continue with business as usual.

Brian Willson recovered, and later, wearing artificial limbs, he returned to the gates of the Concord naval base to join with other veterans in continuing the protest. Once again a group of protestors stood arrayed against an intransigent U.S. Navy.

The maiming of Willson, awful in itself, was also a metaphor for the violent history of the Port Chicago base. The engine of war, though ostensibly directed at enemies abroad, also victimizes, maims, and kills its own at home. The home-front victims at Port Chicago now number in the thousands: the 320 who died in the terrible explosion in 1944; the 390 who were injured; the 258 men imprisoned on the barge, including the 50 who were convicted of mutiny; the thousand or so townspeople displaced from their homes in 1968; the hundreds of peace demonstrators arrested in the 1970s and 1980s; and Brian Willson.

In the course of its history Port Chicago has become a microcosm of questions that face U.S. society: questions of achieving justice at home and ending war abroad. For instance, when the law and social practices themselves are unjust, is it reasonable to expect that justice can be achieved without conflict? The rebellion by the Port Chicago enlisted men, like the civil rights movement and the urban rebellions of the 1960s, was part of a continuum of struggle against racial injustice, an injustice that was institutionalized in segregation laws and discriminatory treatment. That the Port Chicago men who refused to return to work were labeled as "mutineers" is not fundamentally different from the process by which civil rights activists were labeled as "criminals." Where the social structure is unjust, those who actively resist it will be labeled and treated as common criminals. Nevertheless, if the seeds of conflict spring from within the society itself, then any lasting solution requires changes at the source.

This latter consideration was also raised by the Port Chicago peace demonstrations, and it goes to the heart of U.S. foreign policy. Can a foreign policy relying on military intervention hope to succeed in countries where the source of the conflict is internal social contradictions and imbalances? Can U.S. troops and military hardware solve the problems of poverty and exploitation in Vietnam or Central America? The antiwar demonstrators obviously have an answer to these questions, but the nation as a whole remains ambivalent, encouraged by the mass media to believe that where there is conflict there must be outside agitators.

But the agitation may be strictly internal, as also the source of conflict. No outsiders incited the Port Chicago rebellion; and though fifty men were convicted of mutiny and imprisoned, the Navy bureaucracy and the federal government were compelled to admit it was their own policies and practices that were most in need of change.

America would do well to remember Port Chicago.

APPENDIXES

APPENDIX

I

List of the 320 Victims Killed in Port Chicago Explosion, July 17, 1944

IDENTIFIED DEAD

(bodies recovered and identified)

U.S. NAVY AND U.S. NAVAL RESERVE

Officers—U.S. Naval Magazine, Port Chicago:

1. ANDERSON, Maxie Lee
2. CHRISTENBURY, John Boyd
3. JOHNSON, James Basil
4. MORDOH, Gilbert
5. SCHINDLER, Roland
6. WHITE, Raymond Robert
7. WOOD, Harold A.

Enlisted Personnel—U.S. Naval Barracks, Port Chicago:

1. BAILEY, Henry Williams
2. BORN, James Henry
3. BOWDEN, L. T.
4. COFFEE, Eugene Jr.
5. COLEY, Enos
6. GABRIEL, Gerard
7. HAMILTON, A. D.
8. HARRISON, Phillip Harold
9. HILL, Cluster
10. HUDSON, Earl Howard
11. HUGHES, Glen
12. HUGHES, Leroy

13. HUNT, Ross Dee
14. JACKSON, Levi Randol
15. JENNINGS, Willie
16. JOHNSON, Clarence
17. JOHNSON, Gabe
18. JOHNSON, Milton Frank
19. LAW, Willie Jr.
20. LONG, Lemuel McKinley
21. MATHEWS, Lawrence Jr.
22. MAYFIELD, Charles Alvin
23. McFARLAND, Clarence K.
24. MILLER, Otis Kenneth
25. NETTLES, Willie
26. PERSON, Joe Herman
27. SANDERS, Robert
28. SIMS, Willie
29. SMITH, Isaac Ebenezer
30. WALKER, Walter Lee Jr.
31. WARREN, William Claude
32. WASHINGTON, James L.
33. WILLIAMS, Mitchell Adelbert
34. WOODS, James Edward

U.S. MARINE CORPS RESERVE

1. BLANKE, Elwin Arnold

U.S. COAST GUARD RESERVE

1. PORTZ, Edward J.
2. SULLIVAN, James C.

U.S. CIVILIAN CIVIL SERVICE EMPLOYEE OF THE U.S. NAVY

1. ZANARINI, Fred

U.S. MARITIME SERVICE (S.S. *QUINALT VICTORY*)

1. HENRIKSSEN, Elis
2. THOMPSON, Glen E.
3. WIDNER, Louis J.

CIVILIANS

1. BUSTRACK, Lawrence C.
2. HALVERSON, Gunder
3. HUNT, Thomas David

UNIDENTIFIED DEAD

*(men who were on the ships and pier and were missing
and presumed dead after the explosion)*

U.S. NAVY AND U.S. NAVAL RESERVE

Officers—Naval Barracks:

1. BLACKMAN, Thomas L.
2. SHANER, Vernon Carlyle

Armed Guard Officer S.S. E. A. Bryan:

3. HARTMAN, Ralph B.

Enlisted Personnel—U.S. Naval Barracks:

1. AKINS, James Cleo
2. ALLEN, Clarence Jr.
3. ASARE, Leslie Koffic
4. ASH, Isaiah Jr.
5. BACON, David Sr.
6. BAKER, Leonard
7. BARNES, David Jr.
8. BATTLE, Joseph
9. BEASON, Raphel Orval
10. BELL, Silas
11. BLACKWELL, David Edwin
12. BLAYLOCK, Thimon
13. BORDERS, Johnnie C.
14. BOYCE, Charles Louis
15. BREWER, Alvin Jr.
16. BRIDGES, James
17. BROOKS, Walter Lee Jr.
18. BROOME, Johnnie Lee
19. BURNETT, Ernest Lee
20. CALVIN, Wilbert
21. CARLIN, Lawrence Louis
22. CARTER, Robert Andrew
23. CLARK, Eddie Lewis
24. COLEMAN, Bill
25. CONNOR, Arthur Alexander
26. COOLEY, Frank
27. CRAIG, Norman Hamilton
28. CROSS, Eddie Lee
29. CRUMP, Jessie V.
30. CURTIS, Herman Lee
31. DANIEL, Horace Sr.
32. DANSBY, Huby
33. DAVIS, Floyd McKinley
34. DAVIS, Henry Joseph
35. DAVIS, Willie
36. DEVAUGHN, James Lloyd
37. DIXSON, Nathaniel
38. DOYLE, Rayfield David
39. DUNBAR, Herman
40. EBNEZER, Arther Lee
41. EDWARDS, Dunton Ives
42. EDWARDS, Herbert Lee
43. ERVIN, Junios Calvin
44. EUSERY, Luther
45. EVANS, Ananias Sr.
46. EVANS, Horace
47. EVANS, John Henry
48. EVANS, William Lee
49. FELISBRET, John Baptist
50. FERGUSON, Robert Lewis
51. FIELDS, Clarence Sinclair
52. FINNEY, Jessie
53. FORKNER, Matthew Jr.
54. FRANCIS, Joseph Robertson
55. FRANKLIN, Ford Sumpter Jr.
56. FRAZIER, Artie James
57. FROID, Elmer Bertie
58. GAINES, Bennie Lanzie
59. GANT, Elgar
60. GIBSON, John Samuel
61. GILBERT, Jethero
62. GLENN, Samuel
63. GOUDELOCK, Lewis Dennis
64. GRAHAM, Harry Lloyd
65. GREEN, William Henry
66. GRINAGE, Ross Burl
67. HAMILTON, Ernest Eugene
68. HAMM, Emeral
69. HAMMOND, George Russell

70. HANNAH, John Wesley Jr.
71. HARDAWAY, Joe Henry
72. HARDING, John Floyd
73. HARRIS, B. C.
74. HARRIS, Roscoe Alexander
75. HARVEY, Clifford Jr.
76. HAYES, George Washington
77. HAYWOOD, D. C.
78. HECTOR, Douglas Lee
79. HIGGINBOTHAM, David Lee
80. HIGGS, Bobie Richard
81. HILLS, Joseph
82. HITE, Charles William
83. HOLDEN, Rudolph Valenteen
84. HOLLEY, Stanford
85. HOLMES, Eldred Larue
86. HOWARD, Ernest Milton
87. HOWARD, Frank James
88. HUGHES, Theodore Lawrence
89. HUMPHREY, William Jr.
90. HUNT, Wave
91. HUNTER, Rudolph Williams
92. INGRAM, Leroy
93. JACKSON, D. C.
94. JACKSON, James
95. JACKSON, James Edward Mason
96. JACKSON, Paul Eugene
97. JACKSON, Robert Albert Jr.
98. JACKSON, Samuel Jr.
99. JAMISON, Daniel Lucas
100. JOHNSON, Earl Thomas
101. JOHNSON, Harold
102. JOHNSON, Henry Lee
103. JONES, Daniel Lancaster
104. JONES, Ivery Lee
105. JOSEPH, Henry Jr.
106. KEARNEY, Samuel
107. KING, Calvin
108. KING, Clifton
109. LAND, Verna
110. LaPORTE, Sidney Joseph Jr.
111. LAWSON, Cleo
112. LESLIE, Claudius William
113. LEWIS, Aaron Augustus
114. LEWIS, T. C.
115. LYONS, Robert
116. MAKINS, Beattie John
117. MARTIN, Alonzo
118. MARTIN, Rossell Edward
119. MASSIE, Daniel
120. McCLAM, Mitchell
121. MELTON, Calvin
122. MILLER, Ernest Charles
123. MILLER, Ira Jr.
124. MOORE, Marshall Sr.
125. MOORE, Thomas
126. MOORE, William Paul
127. NEAL, Eddie Lue
128. NIXON, James Henry
129. OTEY, William Houston Sr.
130. PACKER, Auguster
131. PASCHAL, William Floyd
132. PEETE, Robert Fulton
133. PERRY, Lester Lee
134. PHILLIPS, Alfred
135. PICKETT, Charles
136. PORTER, Houston
137. PORTER, McCoy
138. POTTS, David William
139. POWELL, Samuel Harry
140. PREUITT, Joe Clarence
141. REID, Arthur Jr.
142. RHODES, James Elton
143. RICHARDSON, Clyde Franklin
144. ROBERTS, James Allen
145. ROBERTS, Mango
146. ROBINSON, Alphonse
147. ROBINSON, Fred Jr.

148. ROGERS, Eugene James
149. SAUNDERS, Wesley
150. SCOTT, Carl Clifton
151. SHECKLES, Joseph Jackson
152. SMITH, James Parker
153. TAYLOR, Ellis
154. TOLSON, Joseph Marcella
155. TOWLES, Maxie Daniel
156. VAN DUNK, Norvin Lester
157. WADE, Isaiah
158. WALKER, Charles Jr.
159. WALKER, Woodrow Luther
160. WASHINGTON, Woodrow Jr.
161. WEST, Daniel
162. WHITE, Joseph Bailey
163. WHITMORE, Arthur
164. WILSON, Maryland Eugene
165. WILSON, Oliver
166. WILSON, Samuel David
167. WRIGHT, Walter Eugene
168. WYATT, Charles

Armed Guard—S.S. **Quinalt Victory:**

169. ALBIN, Jack L.
170. BERGSTROM, Delbert P.
171. BOWMAN, Jack P.
172. HALL, John Gibson
173. HOVLAND, George D.
174. MORROW, Andy
175. MULRYAN, William H.
176. MYERS, Henry J.
177. RIIF, Woodrow A.
178. RISENHOOVER, Jacob D.
179. ROBINSON, William R.
180. ROEDELL, Charles H.
181. ROSE, Jay Jr.
182. ROSS, Otis Kyle
183. SAINT, Woodrow W.
184. SANDERS, Arnold T.
185. SANG, Harold S.

Armed Guard—S.S. **E. A. Bryan:**

186. CAUSEY, Wayland E.
187. CEBELLA, Rudy J.
188. CHASE, Robert E.
189. CHASTAIN, Claude L.
190. GEE, John Jefferson
191. HOLLANDSWORTH, Clarence R.
192. MUIRHEAD, Kenneth H.
193. MULLIGAN, Jesse W.
194. QUICK, Lloyd J.
195. SETZER, Martin J.
196. SINGER, George H.
197. SMALL, Listern L.

U.S. COAST GUARD AND U.S. COAST GUARD RESERVE

1. BRODA, Peter G.
2. DE GRYCE, William G.
3. RILEY, Charles H.

U.S. CIVILIAN CIVIL SERVICE EMPLOYEES OF THE U.S. NAVY

1. HUNNICUTT, Raymond V.
2. MIDDLETON, Harry A.

U.S. MARITIME SERVICE

Crew Members of the S.S. **Quinalt Victory:**

1. BAILEY, Robert D.
2. BARTLETT, Robert E.
3. BELL, John D.
4. BENTLEY, Frederick E.
5. CHENEY, Donald H.
6. CRAWFORD, Hugh E.
7. CRIST, Floyd F.
8. DIEDE, Albert G.
9. DURLAND, Wallace M.
10. EULRICK, Kenneth J.
11. FALOR, Burke E.
12. GARRETT, Eugene W.
13. HENDRICKSEN, Robert K.
14. JUSTESEN, Johannes N.
15. KANNBERG, Walter F.
16. KEIM, Robert E.
17. KOENINGER, Joseph B.
18. MALLERY, Earl L.
19. McDANIEL, Lloyd K.
20. MOEN, Kenneth M.
21. MORELL, Robert S.
22. NARINSKY, Isadore E.
23. NELSON, Roy L.
24. PARSONS, David R.
25. PEARSON, Mike
26. PINSON, Ellis B.
27. POTTER, Richard V.
28. SANDBERG, Virgil R.
29. SCOTT, Albert R.
30. SKANCE, Lester S.
31. SULLIVAN, Howard W.
32. SULLIVAN, Robert J.
33. WILLIAMS, John A.

Crew Members of the S.S. **E. A. Bryan:**

1. ANDRASCHKO, Elmer A.
2. ARSENIAN, Albert A.
3. BENHART, William C.
4. CACIC, Martin M.
5. DAVIS, Ray E.
6. DENONN, Donald L.
7. DORSEY, Thomas E.
8. FALK, George H.
9. FRANKLIN, Marcus J.
10. GILBERT, Alfred L.
11. GILSTRAP, James R.
12. GRANGE, Joseph D. Jr.
13. HAYES, Fred
14. HUTCHINSON, Delbert R.
15. JEPSEN, Peter C.
16. JOHNSON, Charles A.
17. JOHNSON, Clifford R.
18. LANTZ, Ralph A.
19. LOUIS, John A.
20. MALIZIA, Frank C.
21. MANIAGO, Edward
22. NATHAN, Harry E.
23. PORTER, Jesse Sr.
24. ROBERSON, Richard D.
25. SANGSTER, Aaron C. Jr.
26. SHAW, Ellsworth M.
27. SMITH, Howard A.
28. SUCHAN, Andrew
29. TOWNSEND, Robert F.
30. WHITE, Harding E.
31. WITT, George H.

Source: Record of Proceedings of Naval Court of Inquiry, Vol. VIII.

APPENDIX

A Social-Psychological Analysis of the Port Chicago Incident

The Port Chicago story interested me on several levels—the personal, the psychological, and the sociological. Through it I came to feel a personal connection with, and compassion for, my father's generation in a way that I had not before.

From the beginning, as I read the old news clippings and the few other published accounts available, I found myself wondering what social and psychological dynamics had been at work. Clearly there was both a physical explosion and a social explosion. Given that Port Chicago was a segregated base, was the "mutiny" actually an act of protest against discrimination? If so, what social-psychological processes were involved in the emergence of protest among these men? Further, what was the relationship between this incident and larger processes affecting race relations in the Navy and American society in general? From the standpoint of disaster theory the event was also intriguing. The prevailing models of disaster behavior predict a "return to normal" behavior by actors following a disaster. But the Port Chicago explosion was followed by a confrontation involving hundreds of men. What was different about the Port Chicago situation such that the expected behavior trajectory was dramatically altered?

The U.S. Navy, as a military institution, channels or "funnels" individuals through a series of stages (induction, training, duty assignment) whose purpose is to transform the citizen into an effective soldier (Coates and Pellegrin, 287f.). This process is seldom smooth, since civilian values (e.g., the view that one has a right to refuse unreasonable demands) may conflict with military expectations (e.g., the military view that the reasonableness of orders may not be questioned). Individuals may resist and seek to expand their options in the face of the narrowing of behavioral options brought about by the funneling process. In such cases, sanctions of greater or lesser severity will be applied to overcome their resistance.

Thus the role of citizen-soldier has inherent contradictions which may manifest themselves forcefully during periods of stress. Indeed, the Port Chicago events hinted that actions resulting from such contradictions could, at least momentarily, render the military chain of command virtually powerless. Power may inhere in the social structure, but power is also subject to change through social redefinition by actors.

It therefore seemed that the key to understanding the Port Chicago events was to be found in the actors' interpretations of the unfolding situation. The "mutiny," as an instance of collective behavior, could emerge only if there was a consensus, a collective definition of the situation, that allowed the men to act in opposition to the will of the officers. For this reason my sociological interest focused primarily on the black enlisted men at Port Chicago, especially those who engaged in the work stoppage. How did these men perceive and interpret the situations that they encountered? What structural constraints affected the interpretive process? How did a consensus not to return to work emerge within this group?

My interviews with these survivors confirmed that the men were not unaware of the dangers of the work at Port Chicago. Several spontaneously recounted incidents that reflected their recognition of the risks. Some men also described unsafe working practices which increased the danger. It also became clear that the enlisted men had a host of grievances concerning racial discrimination at the base.

I began my coding and analysis of the interviews with no definite hypothesis in mind. I was interested in investigating the processes through which the "mutiny" developed, and I suspected that these would be related to grievances about working conditions. Consequently, as I began coding the interviews, the first categories to emerge fell under such headings as "expectations" (with regard to Navy life), "attitude" (toward officers), "images" (of the work at Port Chicago), "grievances." As I coded and analyzed "grievances," a set of processes for coping with grievances emerged, including "griping," "individual defiance," "confronting," "apathy" ("Nothing can be done"). These were also coded.

Since my sample was small it was not possible to pursue theoretical sampling (Glaser and Strauss, 45f.) to fully elaborate these categories and their properties. I also had no separate comparison group for checking and developing my results. For a time these constraints presented an insurmountable barrier to further analysis.

However, as I reviewed the data I was struck by the apparent lack of significant acts of mass resistance before the explosion. The enlisted men certainly had serious grievances and other matters about which they had long been disturbed, but aside from some individual acts of defiance and one brief work stoppage, there was no evidence of any previous collective action. Why? Was there something in the social structure or social processes at Port Chicago that inhibited such a response? Obviously, the social-structural fact of being in the military implied certain objective constraints on social action. But there was no change in the men's military status before and after the explosion, so this fact was not very helpful as an explanatory variable.

In the literature on social movements and collective behavior there is general agreement that a precipitating incident or problem situation must occur to induce collective action in response (Toch, 7–11; Piven and Cloward, 14; Blumer, 171–79). Indeed, Blumer argues that the social unrest following such a disturbance is characterized by increased excitability and suggestibility of proximate individuals, with the result that the unrest spreads rapidly through the group. Previously established ways of acting now appear as inappropriate or inadequate, and new behavior emerges. Implicit in this model of the emergence of collective behavior is the idea that old modes of behaving or responding are discredited and discarded as new modes appear. The model implies further that the continuation of the old modes of behavior might well preclude the emergence of the new. Thus, the breakdown of the old modes is a logically prior and necessary step in the process of emergent behavior.

This insight proved to be of crucial importance in the analysis of my data. It suggested that for the work stoppage to take place, there must not only have been motivating "grievances," but there must also have been a breakdown in old modes of thinking and behaving which had inhibited collective action to redress the grievances. If such inhibitory processes existed, that would explain why there was no major prior work stoppage. Moreover, this insight also implied that *time* was a critical parameter in my analysis, and that the method of constant comparative analysis (Glaser and Strauss, 105f.) could be applied *before and after* the explosion to the same group of respondents.

I now turned my original research question around and asked what processes could have inhibited the development of a work stoppage before the explosion? Reanalyzing the interview data from this new perspective, I soon "discovered" many descriptions of two social-psychological processes by which the black ammunition loaders, in effect, accommodated themselves to what was in fact a dangerous and disagreeable work situation. Ironically, I had read these descriptions before, but they had no significance until I was sensitized by turning the question around.

The two key processes of accommodation were what I have termed *discounting* and *balancing*. By *discounting* I refer to a process in which the enlisted men came to minimize, to discount, the apparent risks involved in loading munitions. *Balancing* refers to a process by which the men balanced their grievances against the perceived benefits of Navy life. Discounting risks and balancing grievances were coping tactics that served to reduce tension and minimize confrontations between enlisted men and officers over grievances and the dangers of the work.

This is not to imply that discounting and balancing were the only coping tactics that emerged among the enlisted men. There is evidence from my interviews and the documents that some of the men *confronted* the officers with their concerns about working conditions and grievances. Other men went AWOL or engaged in other acts of *individual defiance*. However, all of my informants but one described incidents of discounting and balancing in their experiences at Port Chicago, and I have also found some evidence of these processes in the documentary record.

The enlisted men were confronted with a classic "double bind" situation. They found themselves in a dangerous work situation, while at the same time, because they were under military control, there appeared to be no way to change or get out of the situation. Under such conditions individuals experience cognitive dissonance, a feeling that two experiential elements are in conflict or contradiction. According to Festinger, individuals will seek to reduce dissonance by changing the situation or changing their behavior (including attitudes and opinions) (Festinger, 18–28). Behavioral or attitudinal change will occur if situational change is blocked. This was confirmed by the events at Port Chicago. Locked into a bad situation which could not be changed, discounting and balancing emerged as social processes by which many of the enlisted men changed their perception of the situation and thereby reduced the dissonant stresses they encountered at Port Chicago.

The explosion disrupted these processes by confirming the mortal dangers of the work. It was no longer possible to discount the danger, since the danger had been so horribly demonstrated. As the men talked among themselves in the days following the explosion, a new definition of the situation emerged which asserted that the risks involved in handling ammunition were unacceptable. Moreover, things were made worse by the fact that many of the survivors expected to be granted survivors' leaves to visit their families before being reassigned to regular duty. Such leaves were not granted, creating a major new grievance—and one which could not be balanced by the rapidly diminishing benefits of Navy life.

Thus, from a social-psychological standpoint, my findings indicate that the explosion and its aftermath undermined the coping processes that had enabled the ammunition loaders to tolerate the stresses of a dangerous and difficult working environment. In the postdisaster situation these processes were no longer appropriate, nor were they effective in reducing dissonance. In essence, the coping processes affirmed that "things were not as bad as they appeared." But the awesome explosion and its aftermath showed that in reality things were even worse than they at first appeared, thereby negating the old modes of coping and opening the way for new behavior.

DISCOUNTING AND BALANCING AS COPING STRATEGIES

The major social-psychological finding of my research is that in certain situations of collective stress, discounting and balancing will emerge as important coping strategies. These strategies allow individuals to function in situations that might otherwise be considered intolerable. However, these coping strategies may be disrupted by what Blumer has called an "exciting event" (Blumer, 178)—for example, an explosion—with the result that a new response to the stressful situation emerges: for example, a work stoppage.

Balancing and discounting emerge in situations where individuals experience cognitive dissonance; that is, where they find themselves in some kind of "double bind." For example, in this book it was noted that balancing developed in a situation where the black enlisted men (1) perceived a number of racial inequities in the Port Chicago situation, but (2) believed that nothing could be done to change the situation because of the obstinacy of the military authorities. Consequently, some of these men coped with this dissonance by balancing their grievances against what they regarded as the benefits of Navy life. In this manner, they accommodated themselves to a disagreeable situation.

We may note that in situations of racial accommodation, some form of balancing is often the mechanism by which the victims of racial discrimination accommodate themselves to their condition. Thus, in Booker T. Washington's famous Atlanta Exposition address in 1895, in which he announced his formula for accommodation, Washington in effect urged blacks to balance the acceptance of racial segregation against the presumed economic benefits they would achieve by "casting down their buckets" in the South. In the face of increased racial violence and lynchings, Washington's proposal seemed to many a reasonable way of coping with the collective stress of brutally enforced racial subordination.

Turning to the process of discounting, we saw that discounting emerged in a mandatory work situation where (1) workers knew or suspected that the potential for disaster existed, but (2) the officers (authority) denied the danger and otherwise prevented the situation from being changed. Consequently, some of the enlisted men responded to this dissonance by discounting the risk of explosion—minimizing the danger or trying to blot it from their minds so that they could work as if no danger existed.

Discounting is often encountered in other situations where people must live with the threat of disaster. Coal miners, for example, live with the constant threat of death. One fifty-year veteran of the mines explained how he coped with this stress as follows:

> That slate, it don't have any respect for persons. It'll fall on anybody. It comes to you that the man working right beside you gets killed, say. For a day or two it bothers you, and after that, why, you know you've got a living to make so you go back and try to forget. But I think that 90 percent of the coal miners are scared to death all the time they're in there. You get hurt, you dread going back in there, but you try to forget it—or at least I did, and I don't think anyone is different from what I was. (Quoted in Erikson, 104)

In Figure 1 I have attempted to summarize this discussion of situations in which balancing and discounting emerge as mechanisms for coping with stress.

At Port Chicago the explosion constituted a precipitating event which disrupted the coping processes of discounting and balancing, and opened the way for new responses to the situation. In the

FIGURE 1

1. Perceived grievance(s)

   PLUS   } Balancing

2. Apparent inability to redress

1. Perceived risk

   PLUS   } Discounting

2. Apparent inability to change
   or escape

aftermath of the explosion the men were in a state of shock and, as is common in such situations, there was a widespread fear of a recurrence of the disaster (Wolfenstein, 151). The disaster shattered their coping strategies and left them feeling terrified and demoralized. None of this is unusual. What was unusual about the Port Chicago disaster was that in its aftermath the enlisted men, under the leadership of Joe Small, refused to resume the normal work routine and in effect challenged the military power structure. The implications of these developments for disaster theory and the theory of social power will be examined in the sections that follow.

DISASTERS AND COLLECTIVE STRESS

It will be useful to review the literature on disaster studies to better understand the Port Chicago incident. The concept of disaster has been utilized in diverse and sometimes confusing ways. However, in behavioral science writings there appears to be a convergence in conceptualizations of disaster. Thus, Form and Loomis state that "disasters usually affect entire communities or large segments of communities and are present when the established social systems of the community abruptly cease to operate" (Form and Loomis, 180). Moore characterizes a disaster situation as due to an irresistible force resulting in acute social disorganization (Moore, 733). Somewhat more elaborate is Sjoberg's definition of disaster as "a severe, relatively sudden, and frequently unexpected disruption of normal structural arrangements within a social system, or subsystem, resulting from a force, 'natural' or 'social,' 'internal' to a system or 'external' to it, over which the system has no firm 'control' " (Sjoberg, 357). The convergent aspects of these conceptualizations of disaster are underscored by Robert Merton, who describes disaster as "a sudden and acute form of collective stress . . ." (Merton in Barton, xxiv–xxv).

Common elements in these definitions are the notions of suddenness, acuteness, and collective stress. Barton defines collective stress as referring to situations where "many members of a social system fail to receive expected conditions of life from the system. These conditions of life include the safety of the physical environment, protection from attack, provision of food, shelter, and income, and guidance and information necessary to carry on normal activities" (Barton, 38). There can be little doubt that the events at Port Chicago "fit" this conceptualization of disasters.

What kinds of social behavior emerge in disaster situations? The dominant model of disaster behavior in the literature is a sequential model based on structural-functional theory, and the key concept of social equilibrium. Sjoberg spelled out the implications of this concept for disaster behavior theory:

> . . . A system does seek to sustain some link of working equilibrium among its component parts and/or with respect to its external environment, which includes other systems. And actors in the system generally share some notion of what is normality for it. Yet considerable empirical evidence supports the proposition that both scientists and actors in a system find it exceedingly difficult, often impossible, to discern precisely when and if the system is in equilibrium. Only in extreme situations, when a disaster leads to dramatic deviations from the traditional patterns, will the consensus among actors be that the system is clearly out of kilter. (Sjoberg, 359)

Implicit here is a theory of action in disaster situations: actors become aware that the "system is clearly out of kilter" and they take collective action to restore the social equilibrium. In the case of Port Chicago, we may recall the various tactics employed by the officers—threatening, shaming, reintroducing discounting—in an effort to get the enlisted men to return to work and thereby reestablish the social equilibrium.

The emphasis on restoration of social equilibrium in structural-functional disaster theory led to the development of a time-sequential model for understanding disaster behavior. This model was first worked out in 1952 by J. W. Powell. The model has been widely employed in disaster studies since then, although some researchers, such as Barton, have modified or compressed it. Baker and Chapman summarize the seven phases or periods in the model as follows:

> **1.** WARNING—during which there arises some apprehension based on conditions out of which danger may arise.

2. THREAT—during which people are exposed to communications from others, or to signs, indicating specific, imminent danger.

3. IMPACT—during which the disaster strikes, with consequent death, injury and destruction.

4. INVENTORY—during which those exposed to the disaster begin to form a preliminary picture of what has happened and of their own condition.

5. RESCUE—in which activity turns to immediate help for survivors, first aid for the wounded, freeing trapped victims, fighting fires, etc.

6. REMEDY—during which more deliberate and formal activities are undertaken toward relieving the stricken and their community, both by the survivors and by outside relief agencies that have now moved onto the scene.

7. RECOVERY—during which, for an extended period, the community and the individuals in it either recover their former stability or achieve a stable adaptation to the changed conditions which the disaster brought about. (Baker & Chapman, 7–8)

It is apparent that the first six periods of this model can be "applied"—with some modification—to the Port Chicago disaster. However, it is equally obvious that recovery (of the social equilibrium) did not follow immediately. Rather, a *period of confrontation* ensued (the work stoppage, court-martial, appeals campaign) which eventually resulted in significant social change (desegregation of labor force, establishment of new safety regulations). How and why a period of confrontation may be initiated cannot be explained by the sequential model. Indeed, the sequential model is subject to a criticism that has been made of structural-functional theory in general: it cannot account for social change except as a residual category. The sequential model deals with the social crisis engendered by disaster, but it suggests no processes or mechanisms of disaster behavior that may lead to social change. Change is simply what is left after everything else is explained.

DISASTERS AND SOCIAL CONFRONTATION

This study of the Port Chicago disaster has suggested an important modification of the theory of the social outcome of disaster: a disaster, as a situation of extreme collective stress, may lead to a social crisis which intensifies existing social conflicts or provokes latent conflicts to break into open confrontations. A redefinition of the situation by the survivors of the disaster takes place so that a return to "normality" is precluded.

In the Port Chicago incident a social-psychological crisis was engendered by the traumatic shock of the explosion. Before the explosion the enlisted men had been faced with the stresses of a dangerous and undesirable working situation. These stresses, however, were routinized and made tolerable by the processes of discounting and balancing. The explosion and its aftermath created extreme stresses—a crisis—by disrupting these processes. Through interaction a new definition of the situation emerged among these men which asserted (1) that fear of another explosion due to unsafe working conditions was sufficient reason not to go back to work, and (2) that the officers could not punish the work refusers if everybody "stuck together." The emergence of this new definition of the situation was important in developing solidarity among the enlisted men after the shock and demoralization that followed the explosion. Moreover, this new definition was a major factor in the men's resistance to returning to loading ammunition.

Rue Bucher, in a study of blame and hostility in disasters (Bucher, 1957), has argued that blaming occurs when people are convinced that the responsible agents will not of their own volition take action to prevent a recurrence of the disaster. In the "talking it over" period that followed the Port Chicago disaster, some of the enlisted men came to blame the officers for creating the unsafe working conditions that may have led to the explosion. Many men were also blaming the ammunition itself, the danger of which had been previously discounted. The lack of any official explanation of the cause of the disaster and the failure of the officers to suggest that any changes might be made in the working conditions, or to respond to other grievances, contributed to the blaming process.

Blaming may be regarded, in turn, as part of the larger process of redefining the situation. In *The Derelicts of Company K: A*

Sociological Study of Demoralization, Shibutani presented a relevant model of this process and its outcome:

> **1.** Encounter with a *problematic situation* that calls into question the prevailing institutional norms and definitions.
>
> **2.** *Collective deliberation* by the affected group, during which alternative definitions are put forward and a consensus and common orientation emerge.
>
> **3.** *Coordinated action,* based on the new definition, is taken to resolve the problem. (Shibutani, 426–30)

For the enlisted men at Port Chicago the problematic situation was whether to return to ammunition loading. There was much informal discussion of this problem and there emerged a common orientation not to return to this work. The views expressed by a respected individual (Joe Small) carried special weight in the deliberations. The collective work stoppage was an informally coordinated action taken in hopes of resolving the problem (see Figure 2). Actually the process was somewhat more complicated due to its extension in time. There are tantalizing hints in the research of a complex interplay between deliberation and action as the work stoppage unfolded over several days and the fifty "mutineers" were singled out. It was not simply a matter of deliberation leading to action; sometimes a defiant act—such as the smoking incident in the chow hall—might provoke further discussion and attempts at arriving at (or maintaining) a consensus.

Shibutani developed his model in an effort to conceptualize the process of demoralization in a military unit. He states that demoralization is indicated by the breakdown of discipline within a group and its inability to sustain coordinated action in achieving a goal. From the standpoint of the officers it could be argued that discipline had broken down among the Port Chicago men and they were consequently unable to get on with the job of loading ammunition. But from the standpoint of the enlisted men themselves it could be argued that a *new discipline* was emerging in an effort to achieve a *newly defined* goal—a successful work stoppage. Indeed, there is evidence that as the confrontation intensified, morale among those who continued to resist steadily improved. The pro-

FIGURE 2
DISASTER BEHAVIOR TRAJECTORIES

I. Trajectory predicted by Sequential Model:

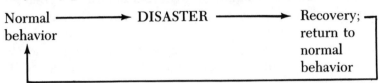

II. Trajectory in Port Chicago disaster:

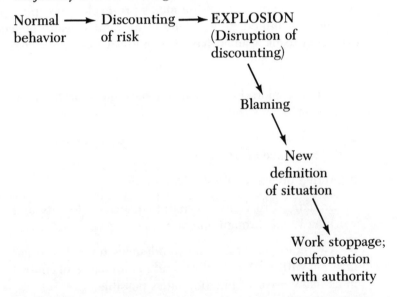

longed process of struggle shaped an aggregate of demoralized individuals into a self-conscious group capable of taking disciplined action. The members of that group came to be known as "the Port Chicago Boys," a label which symbolized and encapsulated the conflict between the enlisted men and the Port Chicago bureaucracy.

MENTAL HEALTH AND COLLECTIVE STRESS

The ability of human beings to cope effectively with situations of extreme stress and crisis has long been of interest to mental health specialists. A number of studies have been made of coping in extreme situations, including Nazi concentration camps (Bettelheim), prisoner of war camps (Biderman), the aftermath of atomic attacks (Janis), and natural disasters (Wolfenstein). These studies reveal the great range of coping strategies that individuals and primary groups may adopt to preserve their mental health in the face of inordinate stresses.

My research into the Port Chicago incident raises questions with regard to the effectiveness of the men's pre-explosion coping processes, and the immediate and long-term mental health effects of the explosion itself. Caplan has identified seven characteristics of effective coping behavior:

1. Active exploration of reality issues and search for information.

2. Free expression of both positive and negative feelings and a tolerance of frustration.

3. Active invoking of help from others.

4. Breaking problems down into manageable bits and working them through one at a time.

5. Awareness of fatigue and tendencies toward disorganization with pacing of efforts and maintenance of control in as many areas of functioning as possible.

6. Active mastery of feelings where possible and acceptance of inevitability where not. Flexibility and willingness to change.

7. Basic trust in oneself and others and basic optimism about outcome. (Caplan, 14)

By this yardstick the efficacy of discounting and balancing must be questioned, since these processes mask reality and constitute a kind of self-deception. On the other hand, these processes psychologically removed the actors and insulated them from the stress-producing factors, thus enabling them to function normally in a stressful environment. Bruno Bettelheim has argued that denial strategies are functionally adaptive in that they are often effective in shielding the individual from a complete realization of the shock in extreme situations (Bettelheim, 48–83). By employing such strategies individuals are able to work and function normally despite the dangers and difficulties they encounter. Indeed, such strategies were of critical importance in "normalizing" the situation at Port Chicago and protecting the enlisted men from massive psychological deterioration and demoralization.

Psychologist Martha Wolfenstein suggests that in predisaster situations minimization of the danger is a normal response. However, she also points out that individuals who have a realistic appreciation of the danger are more likely to survive a disaster with least harm to their mental health (Wolfenstein, 146–7). In this regard, it is noteworthy that the individual (Joe Small) who was able to unite and mobilize the survivors after the explosion was also the individual who several times confronted the officers about the risk of an explosion before the disaster. Because he recognized the danger, perhaps Joe Small was better prepared psychologically to survive and respond to the explosion than those who discounted the danger. By experiencing feelings appropriate to the disaster before it occurred, he was protected from being overwhelmed by its impact.

As is normal in the aftermath of traumatic disasters, many of the survivors experienced shock and disorientation. Fear of recurrence of the disaster was another common (and normal) reaction. However, these reactions were not so severe as to prevent the men from aiding the injured and helping in clearing away debris from the stricken base. There were no recorded instances of nervous breakdown following the explosion, and within days most of the men were back at work with routine barracks chores.

Due to the small size of my sample, it is not possible to make generalizations with regard to the long-term effects of the disaster. Among the men I interviewed I did find some indications of "concentration camp syndrome" (irritability, restlessness, apprehensiveness), which affected survivors of Nazi atrocities (Chodoff, 345–48), but I found little evidence of the "survivor guilt syndrome," which afflicted people who survived atomic disasters (Janis, 377–81). Some respondents were at first reluctant to discuss their experiences with me and expressed concern about possible repercussions to themselves or their families, but given that they were in fact imprisoned for their actions, we must regard this concern as in part reality-based, and not necessarily a sign of psychological imbalance.

Indeed, what is surprising about the men I interviewed is the extent to which they appear not to have been psychically impaired by the trauma they experienced. It is possible that the confrontation (work stoppage) which followed the explosion effectively released tensions and fears which otherwise might have festered and produced mental health problems. Most of the respondents stated that they felt their actions were justified under the circumstances, and that they had no guilt or other misgivings about what they had done. Thus, the confrontation may have been protective of their mental health.

SOCIAL POWER IN THE MILITARY

The Port Chicago rebellion also provides an important insight into the nature of social power. In his famous essay "Class, Status and Party," Max Weber has defined power as "the chance of a man or a number of men to realize their own will in communal action even against the resistance of others who are participating in the action." He adds that law exists "when there is a probability that an order will be upheld by a specific staff of men who will use physical or psychical [ideological] compulsion with the intention of obtaining conformity with the order, or of inflicting sanctions for infringement of it." Power, therefore, appears to inhere in the structure and organization of society and its subunits.

However, the Port Chicago rebellion reveals a situation in which the power of the authorities was eroded and a countervailing locus of power emerged, at least temporarily, among the enlisted men during the process of social interaction.

At first sight, military or police power appears to be the ultimate form of brute power based on physical force. However, a military (or police) unit is effective only so long as the chain of command is intact. That is, orders are issued by those in command and obeyed by those in the ranks. So long as the right of those in command to issue orders is not challenged—or so long as their orders are not viewed as unreasonable—then the chain of command remains intact and orders are obeyed. But this implies that each individual in the chain must at least acquiesce to a definition of the situation that regards specific orders as reasonable and that affirms the right of those higher in the hierarchy to issue commands and have them obeyed.

Fear of sanctions, as Weber suggests, is often the motive for such acquiescence. But even here we must note that there has to be a belief that sanctions can and will be applied in order for fear to become a motive for compliance. What happens when the definition of the situation changes so that there is no longer the belief that sanctions can or will be applied? In that case, as happened in the Port Chicago rebellion, the chain of command breaks down, and with it the effective power of the officers.

Eventually, the officers succeeded in reestablishing the chain of command in a series of confrontations with the enlisted men in which the majority of the men finally came to believe that strong sanctions would be applied to them if they continued their refusal to return to work. Those who did continue to refuse were, in fact, sanctioned by being court-martialed. The power of the officers was thereby restored.

Power, therefore, only partially inheres in the social structure; it also is socially constructed during the process of social interaction which defines the situation for actors. When an event occurs which provokes a redefining of the situation, there may follow a dramatic shift in the locus of power. Indeed, a fundamental and permanent change in the definition of the situation may result in a social movement that effectively changes the social structure (Berger and Luckmann, 92–128). This was the challenge posed by the Port Chicago rebellion—it might have sparked a social movement— and this possibly explains why extreme sanctions—a mutiny court-martial—were employed in suppressing it.

As it was, the Navy tried to break the Port Chicago boys, but it was the Port Chicago men whose action changed the Navy.

APPENDIX

|||

A Note on Sources

Military documents concerning Port Chicago were declassified in 1972 and became available to researchers. The most important primary sources are the Record of the General Court-Martial ("Case of Julius J. Allen, et al.") of the fifty men accused of mutiny, and the Record of the Court of Inquiry that investigated the explosion. Both of these may be found in the archives of the Navy Judge Advocate General's Office in Washington, D.C. The history of the Port Chicago Naval Ammunition Depot may be found in the Administrative Histories of the Twelfth Naval District (copies of which are located in the Navy History Library at the Washington Navy Yard). Records of the construction and reconstruction of Port Chicago are available at the Historical Office of the Naval Construction Battalion at Port Hueneme, California. The Port Chicago War Diary is located in the Operational Archives of the U.S. Naval History Division at the Washington Navy Yard.

The NAACP Legal Defense Fund's involvement in the defense effort is documented in reports and correspondence contained in the archives of the NAACP LDF in New York City and in the NAACP's General Office File, 1940–55, Manuscript Division, Library of Congress. There is also a useful file of Lester Granger's papers in the Manuscript Division, Library of Congress. The General Correspondence Files of Secretary of the Navy James Forrestal contain much valuable material and are located in the Old Army and Navy Branch of the National Archives in Washington. Copies of memoranda sent to President Franklin D. Roosevelt may be found in the Roosevelt Presidential Library at Hyde Park, New York.

Another critical primary source is found in the oral histories that were collected by the author from surviving witnesses and participants in the Port Chicago events.

There is one published book-length account of the Port Chicago disaster and its aftermath. Entitled *No Share of Glory* (Pacific Palisades, Calif., 1964) and authored by Robert E. Pearson, this book was published before many of the primary documents were declassified. The book has serious errors and is not reliable as a source. It also lacks any treatment of the experience of the black enlisted men.

A good brief description of the Port Chicago events was written by Florence Murray in *The Negro Handbook, 1946–47* (New York, 1947). There is also some discussion of it in Dennis D. Nelson, *The Integration of the Negro Into the U.S. Navy* (New York, 1951). More recently, Charles Wollenberg presented a paper on "The Mare Island Mutiny Court-Martial" to the Pacific Coast Branch meeting of the American Historical Association in August 1978. An excellent article based on his paper was published in *California History*, Spring 1979 issue.

Studs Terkel included an interview with Joe Small in his popular oral history of World War II, *The Good War*.

In 1982 I published an article on my Port Chicago research in *The Black Scholar* (Spring issue). In that issue, which I edited, there was also an article entitled "The Last Wave from Port Chicago," by Peter Vogel. Vogel, who then worked as an information officer in the energy research and development programs of the state of New Mexico, presented circumstantial evidence suggesting that the explosion at Port Chicago was nuclear in origin. The article provoked a storm of controversy in the Bay Area press. Eventually, Vogel himself abandoned the theory when no hard evidence could be found to support it.

SOURCES

PRIMARY SOURCES

Interviews with Port Chicago survivors, 1977–85. In possession of the author.

General Correspondence Files, 1944–47, Secretary of the Navy James V. Forrestal. National Archives, Washington, D.C.

General Correspondence Files, 1944, Eleanor and Franklin Roosevelt. Franklin D. Roosevelt Library, Hyde Park, New York.

General Office Files, 1940–55, National Association for the Advancement of Colored People. Manuscript Division, Library of Congress, Washington, D.C.

General Office Files, 1943–45, NAACP Legal Defense and Educational Fund. NAACP LDF Office, New York.

General Office Files (Executive Director), 1944–61, National Urban League. Manuscript Division, Library of Congress, Washington, D.C.

Press Releases, 1944, Twelfth Naval District, Office of Public Relations (typescripts). Federal Record Center, San Bruno, California.

"Record of Proceedings of a Court of Inquiry Convened at the U.S. Naval Magazine, Port Chicago, California," July 21, 1944 (typescript). Navy Judge Advocate General's Office, Washington, D.C.

Trial Transcript, General Court-Martial, "Case of Julius J. Allen, Seaman Second Class, U.S. Naval Reserve, et al.," Sept. 14–Oct. 24, 1944 (typescript). Navy Judge Advocate General's Office, Washington, D.C.

"U.S. Naval Training Center, Great Lakes, Illinois," App. B to Vol. II, *Training Activity, Bureau of Naval Personnel* (typescript). Library, Washington Navy Yard.

"War Time History of U.S. Naval Magazine, Port Chicago, California." In *Bureau of Ordnance, Selected Ammunition Depots*, Vol. II (typescript). Library, Washington Navy Yard.

SECONDARY SOURCES:
Newspapers and Magazines

San Francisco Chronicle
San Francisco Examiner
Oakland Tribune
New York Times

Peoples World
Contra Costa Gazette
Time magazine

SECONDARY SOURCES AND REFERENCES:
Books and Articles

Andrews, Edna May, with Janet Settle, Arliss Harmon, and Takako Endo. *History of Concord: Its Progress and Promise*. Concord, Calif., 1986.

Anonymous. "Mutiny? The Real Story of How the Navy Branded 50 Fear-shocked Sailors as Mutineers." Pamphlet. New York, 1945.

Baker, G.W., and D.W. Chapman. *Man and Society in Disaster*. New York, 1962.

Barbeau, Arthur E., and Florette Henri. *The Unknown Soldiers: Black American Troops in World War I*. Philadelphia, 1974.

Barton, Allan H. *Communities in Disaster*. Foreword by Robert Merton. New York, 1969.

Berger, Peter L., and Thomas Luckmann. *The Social Construction of Reality*. New York, 1967.

Bettelheim, Bruno. *Surviving and Other Essays*. New York, 1979.

Biderman, Albert D. *March to Calumny*. New York, 1963.

Bland, Randall W. *Private Pressure and Public Law: The Legal Career of Thurgood Marshall*. Port Washington, N.Y., 1973.

Blumer, Herbert. "Collective Behavior." In A.M. Lee, *New Outline of the Principles of Sociology*. New York, 1951.

Buchanan, A. Russell. *Black Americans in World War II*. Santa Barbara, Calif., 1972.

Bucher, Rue. "Blame and Hostility in Disaster." *American Journal of Sociology*, Vol. LXII, No. 5 (March 1957).

Caplan, Gerald. *An Approach to Community Mental Health.* New York, 1961.

Chodoff, Paul. "The German Concentration Camp as a Psychological Stress." In Rudolf H. Moos, ed., *Human Adaptation: Coping With Life Crises.* Lexington, Mass., 1976.

Cicourel, Aaron V. *Method and Measurement in Sociology.* New York, 1964.

Coates, Charles H., and Roland J. Pellegrin. *Military Sociology: A Study of American Military Institutions and Military Life.* College Park, Md., 1965.

Cornell, James. *The Great International Disaster Book.* New York, 1976.

Erikson, Kai. *Everything in Its Path: Destruction of Community in the Buffalo Creek Flood.* New York, 1976.

Festinger, Leon. *A Theory of Cognitive Dissonance.* Stanford, Calif., 1957.

Foner, Jack D. *Blacks and the Military in American History.* New York, 1974.

Form, W.H., and C.P. Loomis. "The Persistence and Emergence of Social and Cultural Systems in Disasters." *American Sociological Review,* Vol. XXI, No. 2 (April 1956).

Franklin, John Hope. *From Slavery to Freedom: A History of Negro Americans.* 5th ed. New York, 1980.

Glaser, Barney G., and Anselm L. Strauss. *The Discovery of Grounded Theory.* Chicago, 1967.

Goffman, Erving. *Asylums: Essays on the Social Situation of Mental Patients and Other Inmates.* New York, 1961.

Janis, Irving D. "Aftermath of Atomic Disasters." In Rudolph H. Moos, ed., *Human Adaptation: Coping With Life Crises.* Lexington, Mass., 1976.

Lee, Ulysses G. *The Employment of Negro Troops: The United States Army in World War II.* Washington, D.C., 1966.

MacGregor, Morris J., and Bernard C. Nalty, eds. *Blacks in the United States Armed Forces: Basic Documents.* Vol. VI. Wilmington, Del., 1977.

Merton, Robert K. *Social Theory and Social Structure.* New York, 1968.

Moore, H.E. "Toward a Theory of Disaster." *American Sociological Review,* Vol. XXI, No. 6 (December 1956).

Morgan, Ted . *FDR: A Biography.* New York, 1985.

Mullen, Robert W. *Blacks in America's Wars.* New York, 1973.

Murray, Florence. *The Negro Handbook.* New York, 1947.

Nalty, Bernard C. *Strength for the Fight: A History of Black Americans in the Military.* New York, 1986.

Nelson, Dennis D. *The Integration of the Negro Into the U.S. Navy.* New York, 1951.

Pearson, Robert E. *No Share of Glory.* Pacific Palisades, Calif., 1964.

Piven, Frances Fox, and Richard A. Cloward. *Poor People's Movements: Why They Succeed, How They Fail.* New York, 1977.

Quarantelli, E.L., ed. *Disasters: Theory and Research.* Beverly Hills, Calif., 1978.

Rapoport, Roger. "Port Chicago." *West* magazine, *Los Angeles Times,* Aug. 18, 1968.

Reddick, L.D. "The Negro in the United States Navy During World War II." *The Journal of Negro History,* Vol. XXXII, No. 2 (April 1947).

Sawyer, L.A., and W.H. Mitchell. *The Liberty Ships.* 2nd ed. London, 1985.

Schatzman, Leonard. "A Sequence Pattern of Disaster and Its Consequences for Community." Ph.D. diss., 1960.

Schatzman, Leonard, and Georgia Adams. "The Calculus and Management of Risk: The Case of Pregnancy and Abortion." Unpublished, n.d.

Shibutani, Tomatsu. *The Derelicts of Company K: A Sociological Study of Demoralization.* Berkeley, Calif., 1978.

Sjoberg, Gideon. "Disasters and Social Change." In G.W. Baker and D.W. Chapman, *Man and Society in Disaster.* New York, 1962.

Sorokin, P.A. *Man and Society in Calamity.* New York, 1942.

Terkel, Studs. *"The Good War": An Oral History of World War II.* New York, 1984.

Toch, Hans. *The Social Psychology of Social Movements.* New York, 1965.

Wolfenstein, Martha. *Disaster: A Psychological Essay.* Glencoe, Ill., 1957.

Wollenberg, Charles. "Black vs. Navy Blue: The Mare Island Mutiny Court Martial." *California History*, Spring 1979.

Wynn, Neil. *The Afro-American and the Second World War.* New York, 1975.

ABOUT THE AUTHOR

Robert L. Allen is the author of two previous books: *Black Awakening in Capitalist America* (Doubleday, 1969; reissued by Africa World Press, 1989) and *Reluctant Reformers: Racism and American Social Reform Movements* (Howard University Press, 1974; reissued 1983). For eleven years he was an editor of *THE BLACK SCHOLAR* magazine. He also taught sociology and ethnic studies at San Jose State University and Mills College in Oakland, California. A graduate of Morehouse College in Atlanta, Georgia, he holds a Ph.D. in sociology from the University of California, San Francisco. Allen has both observed and actively participated in the civil rights and antiwar movements of the past twenty-five years. He lives in Oakland, California and works on the staff of the Oakland Men's Project.

INDEX